"One of the things I love about these books is that they are so accessible to every aspiring writer."

— RICK LUDWIG, AUTHOR OF *MIRRORED*

"I reread these books before I start each book I write."

— CALLIE HUTTON, *USA TODAY*-BESTSELLING AUTHOR OF *FOR THE LOVE OF THE VISCOUNT*

"Bernhardt shows you exactly what makes literary characters keep people interested and how to use those strengths when creating characters of your own."

— R.J. JOHNSON, AUTHOR OF *THE TWELVE STONES*

"Easy to read while delivering good material with some occasional humor."

— DAVID SULLIVAN, AUTHOR

"This book gives everything that it promises. And all the other writing books written by William Bernhardt are on my wish list."

— C.H. SCARLETT, AUTHOR

THINKING THEME

The Heart of the Matter

WILLIAM BERNHARDT

BABYLON
BOOKS

Dedicated to all the Red Sneaker Writers:
You can't fail unless you quit.

You can't have any kind of a story without having some kind of a theme, something to say between the lines.

Robert Wise

CONTENTS

INTRODUCTION

If this is not your first Red Sneaker book, or if you've attended Red Sneaker retreats or conventions, you can skip to Chapter One. If you're new, let me take a moment to explain.

I've been telling stories for several decades, doing almost every kind of writing imaginable. I've been speaking at workshops and conferences almost as long. Every time I step behind the podium I see long rows of talented people frustrated by the fact that they haven't sold any books. Yes, the market is changing and agents are hard to find and self-publishing can be challenging. But when aspiring writers work hard but still don't succeed...there's usually a reason. Too often enormous potential is lost due to a lack of fundamental knowledge. Sometimes a little guidance is all that stands between an unknown writer and a satisfying writing career.

I've seen writing instructors and writing texts that seem more interested in appearing literary than in providing useful information. Sometimes I think presenters do more to obfuscate the subject than to explain it. Perhaps they feel that if they make the writing process as mysterious as possible, it will make them seem profound—or perhaps they don't understand the subject well themselves. Some of the best writers I know are not particularly good teachers, because they've never thought consciously about the creative process.

Hoping to be more useful, I founded the Red Sneaker Writing Center. Why Red Sneakers? Because I love my red sneakers. They're practical, flexible, sturdy—full of flair and fun. In other words, they're exactly what writing instruction should be. Practical, dynamic, and designed to unleash the creative spirit, to give the imagination a platform for creating wondrous work.

I held the first Red Sneaker Writers conference in 2005. I invited the best speakers I knew, people who had published many books but also could teach. Then I launched my small-group writing retreats—intensive days working with a handful of aspiring writers. The retreats gave me the opportunity to read, edit, and work one-on-one with people so I could target their needs and make sure they got what would help them most. This approach worked well and I'm proud to say a substantial number of writers have graduated from my programs, published, and even hit the bestseller lists. But of course, not everyone can attend a retreat.

This book, and the other in this series, are designed to provide assistance to writers regardless of their location. The books are short, inexpensive, and targeted to specific areas where a writer might want help.

Let me see if I can anticipate your questions:

Why are these books so short? Because I've expunged the unnecessary and the unhelpful. I've pared it down to the essential information, useful ideas that can improve the quality of your writing. Too many instructional books are padded with excerpts and repetition to fill word counts required by book contracts. That's not the Red Sneaker way.

Why are you writing several different books instead of one big book? I encourage writers to commit to writing every day and to maintain a consistent writing schedule. Sometimes reading about writing can be an excuse for not writing. You can read the Red Sneaker books without losing much time. In fact, each can be read in an afternoon. Take one day off from your writing. Make notes as you read. See if that doesn't trigger ideas about how you might improve your writing. Then get back to work.

You reference other books as examples, but you rarely quote excerpts. Why?

Two reasons. First, I'm trying to keep these books brief. I will cite a book as an example, and if you want to look up a particular passage, it's easy enough to do. You don't need me to cut and paste it for you. Second, if I quote from materials currently under copyright protection, I have to pay a fee, which means I'd need to raise the price of the book. I don't want to do that. I think you can grasp my points without reading copyrighted excerpts. Too often, in my opinion, excessive excerpting is done to pad the page count.

Why does each chapter end with exercises?

The exercises are a completely integrated and essential part of the book, designed to simulate what happens in my small-group writing retreats. Samuel Johnson was correct when he wrote: *Scribendo disces scribere.* Meaning: You learn to write by writing. These principles won't be concretized in your brain until you put them into practice.

So get the full benefit from this book. Complete the exercises. If you were in one of my retreats, this would be your homework. I won't be hovering over your shoulder as you read this book—but you should do the exercises anyway.

What else does the Red Sneaker Writers Center do?

We send out a free e-newsletter filled with writing advice, market analysis, and other items of interest. If you would like to be added to the mailing list, please visit my website. We also have a free bi-weekly Red Sneaker podcast with all the latest news and interviews with industry professionals. I host an annual conference, WriterCon, over Labor Day weekend and small-group writing retreats throughout the year. There will be future books in this series. And we sponsor a literary magazine called *Conclave* that would love to see you submit your poems, short fiction, and creative nonfiction. Our Balkan Press publishes books, primarily fiction and poetry.

Okay, enough of the warm-up act. Read this book. Then write your story. Follow your dreams. Never give up.

William Bernhardt

THOUGHTS ON THEME

"The theme, what's behind the emotion, the meaning, all that comes later."

— STANLEY KUBRICK

In the Red Sneaker Book Series, this volume is an outlier. It differs from all the other books in the series, and in some respects, even contradicts some of the Great Nuggets of Wisdom I've delivered in those earlier entries. That should give you some idea just how different theme is from the previous topics.

For instance, all the previous books in the series have emphasized the importance of pre-planning, pre-writing, and outlining. Look before you leap, basically. Think about this massive novel-length project before you spend several years rolling around in it. But theme is different. You can't start a novel without having some idea what's going to happen, and you can't plunge into that first paragraph without having some idea who your primary character is. But it is perfectly possible to start a book without fully realizing what the central theme might be. In fact, that might be the best way to do it.

Many times I've started a book and been well into the writing before I fully understood what I was writing about. I knew what the plot threads were, and I knew who the protagonist and antagonist would be. But the thematic details remained elusive. When you're just getting started, particularly if this is a work of popular fiction, you are probably best served by giving your initial focus to telling a good story. Later, additional layers may present themselves, once your subconscious mind is fully immersed in the tale you're telling.

One of the early books in my Ben Kincaid series happened like that. In *Cruel Justice*, I told a story (suggested to me by a judge who handled a similar case) in which Ben tackles the defense of a developmentally disabled young man accused of murder. This case also involves Ben with a high society sort who wants to be a good father—but doesn't know how. Ben's friend Mike has to save his ex-wife's son—apparently not realizing the child is his own. And Ben learns some startling truths about his deceased father. But it was several drafts into the book before I thought—

Wait.

Never mind what's happening with the murders and the courtroom and such. This book is about fatherhood. Which shouldn't have surprised me, since my first son had been born shortly before.

There was just one problem. The parent who brought the case to Ben's attention, who schemed and connived to get Ben to take the case—was the young man's mother.

That got changed in a hurry, once I realized what this book was about. The mother became a father, which worked better anyway. And when the review came out from *Publishers Weekly*, there was nothing but praise. They called it "…Bernhardt's rumination on good fathers, bad fathers, and fathers never known."

I almost cried. I distinctly remember thinking this was the

best book in the series. In fact, I thought it was the best work I'd done to date, period.

More recently, I completed the nineteenth Ben Kincaid novel (time flies when you're having fun). And once again, it was several drafts into the writing process before I realized what I was writing about. I was sitting in an airport restaurant, waiting for my delayed flight to depart, reading someone else's book, when the central idea bubbled up to the surface of my brain. *You didn't bring Ben's sister back just for continuity's sake*, a voice said. *You did it because they have unfinished business.* And I realized that was the emotional core of the story. Once the book's theme came together, I had the ammunition I needed to deepen the characters and enrich the plot.

In *Excellent Editing*, I explained that writing is a process with many steps, none of which can be skipped without weakening the finished project. This is a good example of the importance of this process. If I'd rushed to the finish line, raced to meet a deadline, the theme might never have emerged. The acclaimed short story writer, Alice Munro, said, "I never start out with any kind of connecting theme.... Everything just falls the way it falls." And yet, every day, literature students analyze her work and write lengthy papers analyzing her themes. Those themes are there. She just let them reveal themselves naturally.

Let theme emerge during the writing process.

If this notion doesn't make sense to you, it may be because we have different ideas about what constitutes theme. So let me tell you what I think theme is—and what it isn't.

THE SILVER CHALICE

SOME WRITERS' IDEAS ABOUT THEME HARKEN BACK AN EARLY middle-school English class where a well-intentioned teacher tried to get students to appreciate a complex book they were possibly not yet ready for. As a result, instead of appreciating the book, it seemed as if the teacher was beating it to death with a rubber hose. "What does it mean?" This too often devolves to "Give me the secret message encoded in this text. There can be only one." And that secret message is the theme.

Here's what I think. Books are not cryptograms, and theme is not a secret meaning the author has secreted in the text. I suspect that in many cases authors are not even consciously aware of their theme—but that doesn't mean it isn't there. It's also a mistake to think of theme as some ponderous Moral of the Story. That's not the way it usually works, at least not in the works we remember best. Sure, in Aesop's Fables, each little tale leads to the Moral. Slow and steady wins the race, etc. And that's why we think of these as children's stories. Because they are too obvious and simple to intellectually engage an adult.

To me, the best use of theme is considerably subtler. Theme is not an overt message you impose upon your story. Theme is the container for your story. Theme is the golden punch bowl, or goblet, or chalice. It holds all the other elements in place—but also enhances them, makes them richer and deeper and more coherent than they might otherwise be.

Granted, that chalice may go completely unnoticed by some readers, and you know what? That's fine. My first novel, *Primary Justice*, has a scene near the end, after the mystery has been solved, when Ben visits his mother and resolves some pending psychological baggage. One of my earliest unintended readers, a co-worker who found the manuscript on my desk and read it pre-pub, told me she liked the book— "But what was the point of that scene at the end with Ben's mother?" I thought that scene was the key to the whole story, but she thought it completely superfluous, since it didn't relate to the mystery. I'm not implying that she wasn't bright—she simply read for different reasons.

Not everyone will grasp your theme—but it will elevate the story for those who do.

Anytime you put anything in your book that resembles subtlety, there's a chance that some reader might miss it. That doesn't mean you shouldn't bother. Different readers read for different reasons. If you've provided an entertaining tale full of twists and revelations, and the reader enjoyed it, you've done your job. On the other hand, if you've told a terrific story but also given it a little added oomph, something to think about, something to take away, something to enrich and make it more meaningful—then you've done even more. You've created a story of higher and possibly enduring value. And I guarantee *someone* will get it. Even if it's not the temp. The chalice may go unnoticed by some, but it's still there. For those readers who appreciate such things—and there are many—it's the Holy Grail of reading.

SHARPENING THE FOCUS

I WANT TO DISABUSE YOU OF THE IDEA THAT THEME IS A PONDEROUS overlay, or perhaps shroud, that you impose on your story, whether it likes it or not, because you want to seem more literary. I do not think the key to success is creating elliptical themes that can only be teased out with repeated readings and scholarly research. There are those who might differ. Explaining his later work, James Joyce famously said, "I've put in so many enigmas and puzzles that it will keep the professors busy for centuries arguing over what I meant, and that's the only way of ensuring one's immortality." This approach may inspire dissertations, but I'm not sure it inspires much love. I haven't noticed anyone reading *Finnegan's Wake* on an airplane, and I don't think that's likely to change any time soon.

Forget about trying to create an insulating blanket to amuse academics and critics. Storytelling is not a game of hide and seek. Yes, you should have a theme, but not to validate your work or show how smart you are. The theme should give the story sharper focus, like slowly turning the lens until you've found the correct f-stop. Like so much in the world of writing, this is easier to say than to do, but if you can pull it off, it's the best possible way to distinguish your work. There may be other competent novels and there may be other writers who can create decent characters and fast-paced plots. But books with genuine thematic strength are relatively rare.

Theme isn't about taking a picture. It's about sharpening the focus on the picture that's already there.

What James Joyce didn't get, and some of his acolytes also miss, is that we admire his work because he was a daring innovator who chose words carefully and had something to say. The wordplay and cryptic allusions may enhance the read for some, but if that's all there was, his work would have disappeared quickly. You should use theme to enhance, not to mystify. You should use it to prevent your book from being quickly discarded and forgotten. You should use it to prevent readers from thinking, Well, that was nice, but what did it matter? People remember books that have strong thematic content, something to say, something to move, stimulate, or inspire. Those books are recommended, not discarded. You want people to recall your story a week later, a month later, a year later. You want them telling their friends: Wow, I can't stop thinking about that book!

Discovering your Purpose

In *Story Structure*, I defined "structure" as "the selection of events from characters' lives strategically arranged to serve the writer's purpose." The whole concept of achieving "the writer's purpose," of course, means that you had some purpose in mind when you embarked upon this perilous journey. First and foremost, you must possess a driving need to tell a story, to create a fictional world, to take part in the Great Conversation. I don't think it's possible to survive all the slings and arrows of publication otherwise.

But there was probably more to it than just that, wasn't there?

When writers are interviewed, they often become self-conscious or insecure. Popular fiction writers rarely find themselves being praised by the *New York Times* book reviewer or short-listed for the Pulitzer. You may hear them intimate that they are only writing for money. I heard a writer friend say on a panel, "This is a game and the score is kept with dollar bills." Well, fine, everyone likes to have money in the bank, but then again, there are simpler and more dependable ways of making money than writing. Actually, all the ways of making money are simpler and more dependable than writing. So what inspires us to take up the pen and start down this difficult road?

Every book should have a good reason for being written.

I have often said that I don't believe there's anything genetic about writing ability. It's not encoded in our DNA. When people talk about someone being a "born writer," they're usually talking about being born with the drive, not the ability. That's a key distinction. The way to become a good writer is to read voraciously, study the craft, and practice, practice, practice. Write and then write some more, because like every other endeavor in life, the more you do the better you get. Remember Malcolm Gladwell's "10,000 hours" rule? You put in 10,000 hours practicing to be a writer (or anything else), and you'll emerge a world-class talent. Most aspiring writers never come close to that investment of time, including many who obtain some level of success.

But some people are born with the drive, or develop it when they're still young and impressionable. That's why most of the time, when people are honest, they will admit to thinking about being a writer when they were young, perhaps the first time they read a book that moved them, changed their way of thinking, left them feeling inspired or transformed or better than they were before. That level of passion is rare, and if it is nurtured, encouraged, and pursued, often leads to great accomplishments.

But at some point in this journey, the writer almost certainly acquires an additional realization: They have something to say.

A writer must have something to say.

Ever feel like you have something pent up inside you that's got to get out, something you've got to communicate, something you want everyone in the world to know? Of course you do. Many people in many fields are infected with this near-messianic impulse. It might lure someone into a career in politics or public service. It could lead someone to becoming a fundraiser, advocate, lobbyist, firefighter, or teacher. But what I've seen over and over again is how this zeal draws the best and brightest into the arts—music, architecture, filmmaking, painting—including the art closest to my heart, writing.

As you will read in subsequent chapters, I recommend avoiding overt political messages, but several of my books have addressed and acknowledged the existence of complex political dilemmas. *Death Row* involves a man who has been on death row for years, although Ben believes he is innocent. Hard to read that story without dwelling on whether the death penalty, the ultimate sanction, can be justified when our justice system is so flawed. I'm proud to say that I've received mail from readers saying that book changed their position on this issue. Similarly, I've written two books that gravitated around LGBT issues, the first of which, *Hate Crime*, was written almost twenty years before the Supreme Court legalized gay marriage. Gay rights were not nearly so well accepted then as now, but I'm proud that many readers saw my books as leading the charge, addressing issues other thriller writers wouldn't touch. Granted, when you tackle controversial issues, you risk alienating someone, but as long as you dramatize, rather than polemicize, most readers will accept it, and it might give your story more heft.

Writing is both an art and a skill, and you need to master both if you hope to succeed. Most of the Red Sneaker books have concerned themselves with the craft of writing, because that's something that can be taught. Art is more elusive. But I told you up front this book would be different from the others in the series. Because this book is about art. Theme is about art.

When you want to take your work to the next level, you won't do it by writing more poetically, using more (or fewer) adjectives, rejecting happy endings, ditching quotation marks, or any other showy devices. You'll do it by writing a book that has something to say. You're not coming down off Sinai to deliver the Truth. You're whispering in the ear of those special people who have chosen to spend a few hours with your story. This is more like communion than revelation. This is a special relationship between writer and reader, and it's something that exists nowhere else, at least not in the same way.

Might your book survive without theme? Yes. But theme is your path to greatness. It's your Letter from Hogwarts, your Golden Ticket wrapped in a candy bar, and not everyone gets one, so let's make sure you make the most of yours, shall we?

Read on.

HIGHLIGHTS/EXERCISES

Highlights

1) Let theme emerge during the writing and revision process.

2) Not everyone will grasp your theme—but it will elevate the book for those who do.

3) Theme isn't about taking a picture. It's about sharpening the focus on the picture that's already there.

4) Every book should have a good reason for being written.

5) A writer must have something to say.

Red Sneaker Exercises

1) Why do you want to write a book? Or, if you've done this before, why are you writing another book? There are easier things to do. What drives you to ascend this daunting mountain? What is it you crave most? Fame? Fortune? Literary acclaim? If

your books could accomplish anything, for you or others, what would it be?

2) Now that you know what you'd like to achieve, think about how you might accomplish that through a work of fiction. What kind of story should you tell?

3) After you've finished the third draft of your work-in-progress, get in a comfortable chair, put on some pleasant but non-distracting music (probably something without lyrics) and think about your book. What have you been writing about? What's the common thread? Let your mind wander. Free associate. Think about the books that have been your favorites over the years. Even if you're not consciously trying, you might make a connection. You might uncover the angle that makes this book even more special than you imagined when you began the project.

4) John Lennon started with a fairly simple idea: Wouldn't the world be better if we didn't have so much to fight about? That led to he and Yoko imagining a world without so many points of contention…and that led to one of the most beautiful songs ever written, a song that is brilliant in its simplicity, a song that all around the world is cherished and treated more like an anthem than a pop tune. What ideas do you cherish? How will you write about them?

2

THE MORALITY OF FICTION

"Even frothy entertainment is not harmed by a touch of moral responsibility, at least an evasion of too fashionable simplifications."

— JOHN GARDNER

All stories inevitably convey society's underlying priorities, assumptions, and values. There's no way around this. And why would you want to? You live in the world, you write in the world, your books are bound to be part of it. You may pointedly reject some of society's prevailing values, but your stories are still in and of it.

It has always been so. When we look back at the oldest surviving stories, we find tales of heroic adventure that were obviously intended to instill noble sentiments, fan nationalistic fervor, or explain the ways of the universe as best anyone could in a pre-scientific era. *The Aenied* created an appealing fable to give Romans a sense of history and purpose. *The Odyssey* used supernatural deities to explain the unexplainable, why we have plagues, earthquakes, tidal waves, and worst of all, war.

I have always found pleasure in reading books not only set in but written in the past. (My Masters specialty field was Victorian Literature and my Masters paper was on *Alice's Adventures in Wonderland*.) When you read something set in an earlier era, you gain insight into how people of that time lived and thought—which may turn out to be not all that different from how you and your friends live and think. This is why writers such as Jane Austen, who wrote about her time and the people in it, remain so enduringly popular. Society may change, technology may change, but people—they haven't changed all that much and maybe never will. What motivated people two hundred years ago is still essentially what motivates people today. We love stories in part because they remind us who we are and what matters to us.

Stories are the glue that binds us together and gives meaning to our fragile existence.

ALL FICTION HAS VALUE...AND VALUES

WE TEND TO BE DRAWN TO CERTAIN KINDS OF BOOKS. SOMETIMES it's a setting we find appealing. Sometimes it's the discussion of an intriguing issue or idea. Sometimes it's a charming fantasy world. Sometimes it's the spirit of adventure, of teamwork, of camaraderie. If there's a kind of book that automatically interests you, even before you know much about it, you might consider writing something in that vein yourself. You have an edge, an inside track. If it appeals to you, it likely will appeal to others as well.

In the 90s, legal thrillers surged. I think this was spurred by an interest in understanding the wheels of justice, how they turn, who turns them, why things happen the way they do. And in part, the prevailing cynicism about lawyers caused some readers to seek books that presented similarly cynical views. I might have sold more books if Ben Kincaid had not been such a swell guy. But I also think part of the ongoing appeal of the series is that Ben represents the lawyer everyone wishes they had—but can't seem to find in the real world.

Techno-thrillers appeal to those who favor strong shows of military force. In the wake of 9/11, many writers played on the anti-Middle Eastern sentiment and wrote thrillers with evil robed sheiks plotting world domination to impose sharia law on those naïve democracies. Science fiction appeals to those who believe in science, and are interested in how technology will influence our future. Religious fiction appeals to those who are or want to be spiritual people. And romances appeal to those who still believe in love—even if it's absent from their present life. Fiction can fill gaps, but only if it presents a worldview that is shared by the reader.

Readers are drawn to books that address issues that interest them or reinforce their preexisting beliefs.

Some may read to have their values challenged, but I suspect they are in the minority. If you can change someone's mind with your story, you've truly made your mark. I mentioned a few instances when my books altered the way people thought. In part, they stick in my mind because they are infrequent. Still, the books that change the way you think may be more likely to remain with you after the reading is finished. Harriet Beecher Stowe pulled off that stunt—in *Uncle Tom's Cabin*—and the history of a nation was altered. She was far from the first to address the horrors and inequities of slavery, but her approach was different. Instead of preaching or lecturing, she dramatized the plight of the slave, the hard hours, the severed families, the cruelties and abuses of slave masters. Story proved more powerful in changing attitudes than sermonizing or delivering overt morals.

You are probably more likely to attract an audience with a theme that targets readers seeking reinforcement for what they already believe, or people feeling an emptiness in their lives they hope to fill. Many spiritual or inspirational books have promised insight and wisdom, but traded on vagueness and platitudes. When I was young, one of the most popular books around was *Jonathan Livingston Seagull*, a photo gallery of birds in flight with a vague parable attached. In my mind, the strength of the tale lay in the fact that it was so opaque readers could make it mean anything that appealed to them.

In more recent times, *The Celestine Prophecy* offered similarly nebulous wisdom. I sat on a three-hour flight once watching a reader use a yellow marker to highlight the bold-faced nuggets of wisdom in this arcane text. The book promises nine great insights—though after the book became a bestseller, it turned out there were several more for sequels. I may be in a minority, but I felt disappointed when I finally read the gigantically popular *Tuesdays With Morrie*, a dialogue with a teacher who offered insights such as "Devote yourself to loving others." Really? My mother covered this when I was five.

Readers are drawn to books that fill needs or promise elusive wisdom.

There's money to be made by offering spiritual insight—or starting your own *Dianetics*-type religion—but I don't think that's the path to great literature. A better approach would be to strive for a strong story that exemplifies an important theme, without clubbing readers over the head with it. There is nothing radical about this suggestion. It only exemplifies what has been true since the dawn of storytelling: all fiction is moral. When we create stories, we stand in a time-honored tradition of using fiction to exemplify a worldview worth sharing. So let's talk about the best possible way to do that.

ON MORAL FICTION

·   ·   ·

I WILL READILY ADMIT THAT MY THOUGHTS ON THIS SUBJECT ARE heavily influenced by a book I read decades ago when I was a young and aspiring writer: *On Moral Fiction* by John Gardner. This book was controversial when released, in an era of shifting values and "If it feels good, do it." Talking about morality had fallen out of favor, especially in the artistic community, and Gardner took a lot of grief for it. But to me, this book, essentially a long, well-reasoned essay, took storytelling back to its roots. In reality, storytelling had never left its roots. Some of its practitioners had simply forgotten the point of the exercise.

Gardner argued that, "True art is moral. We recognize true art by its careful, thoroughly honest search for an analysis of values." To me, this was an academic way of saying that stories show us the path, the way, how we ought to live, how we ought to interact with one another. It's important to realize that when Gardner wrote about morals, he did not promote a particular viewpoint, religion, or cultural ideal. He took the broader view. To Gardner, storytelling should aspire and inspire. Fiction should aim to help the reader uncover the human values that are universally worthy. And it should accomplish this, not by telling the reader what those values are, but by helping readers discover values for themselves.

Stories are inherently moral, and should help readers discover larger truths.

You won't be surprised to hear that Gardner specifically addressed the concept of theme. "By theme we mean not a message—a word no good writer likes applied to his work—but the general subject, as the theme of an evening of debates may be Worldwide Inflation." In other words, theme is about saying, Look, this is an important topic. Let's think seriously about it. Let's avoid reactionary responses or imitation and instead give this genuine contemplation. At the end of such an inquiry, readers may find penetrating themes that illuminate their lives.

This was the approach I took in the two books I mentioned

before involving LGBT issues. Instead of telling people what to think, I tried to suggest what to think about. The same was true in *Capitol Conspiracy*, an obvious response to the Patriot Act, or more recently, *Justice Returns*, a response to more recent phenomena such as the USA Freedom Act, waterboarding, "enhanced interrogation techniques," NSA eavesdropping, and other modern-day privacy invasions. The question I hoped to pose was, What kind of nation do we want to be? What values take priority? And then let readers answer the questions themselves.

Theme should focus readers' attention on important questions—without attempting to force answers.

Gardner was not the first to suggest this approach. In an earlier era, Anton Chekov, not only a great writer but a great writer about writing, said "a writer does not solve a problem so much as state the problem correctly." Dickens was arguably less subtle, but you can't read great novels like *Oliver Twist* and *Nicholas Nickleby* without understanding that he is urging readers to take a long hard look at the world—and to consider whether it could be improved. Surely everyone has read *A Christmas Carol*, or seen one of the endless adaptations. Dickens takes us through the rapid-fire reformation of a miser who eventually realizes that if all he ever cares about is money, he'll end up in an unmarked grave with no one mourning his passing. It's hard to read the book without wondering whether you should begin correcting the errors of your own life—before it's too late.

In *Story Structure*, I recommended an exercise in which readers identify their three favorite books, those that they have loved most. I've heard from many who have done it, looking for connections, trying to uncover the issues most prominent in their subconscious. Author Sylvia Day once wrote, "If you can't figure out what a writer's theme is, look at the books you're attracted to." Good advice. More often than not, what people have found is a common theme linking their three books together—but not necessarily a message. They may be drawn to books concerning broken homes, absent fathers, man vs. nature, reason vs. emotion, sin vs. redemption--which means there's a good chance any book they write will address the same issue. This may emerge unconsciously—but you're likely to do it better if you can bring it to the mental forefront, so you can integrate it thoroughly in your story.

EMULATING THE GREATS

WHICH ARE THE BOOKS THAT HAVE HAD THE MOST IMPACT ON readers throughout the ages? I've already mentioned the effect *Uncle Tom's Cabin* had on American history. Similarly, books like *The Great Gatsby* and *The Adventures of Huckleberry Finn* loom large in American libraries and literary reading lists. Why? *Gatsby* was considered a flop when first released, but it gained steam over time. Now people see it as Fitzgerald directing attention to the so-called American Dream. Jay Gatsby, after all, has raised himself from humble beginnings to a position of opulence, envy, and wealth. Did it make him happy? No. He's obsessed with the one thing (of dubious value) that he didn't get—Daisy.

Huck Finn has been heavily criticized. When first released, it received scorn because of the local dialect Twain employed. More recently, *Huck* has been controversial because that local dialect involves racist terms common in Twain's boyhood but thankfully out of favor today. The story involves a poorly educated boy struggling to reconcile the conflict between what society tells him is right and what, after he has spent some time with an escaped slave, his heart tells him is right. Both books involve fundamental issues, primal conflicts between the world and the people who must live in it.

Great books address great themes.

War and Peace announces its epic theme in the title. You may not be surprised to hear that, of the two, "Peace" is preferred. *Pride and Prejudice* is equally up front about theme. He's proud and she's prejudiced, and they'd both better get over it or they're never going to find happiness together. George Orwell gave us overtly political cautionary tales in *Animal Farm* and *1984*. Huxley warned that we would be enslaved, not by fascism, but by pleasure, in *Brave New World*—and his future looks much more like the present-day world than Orwell's does. My favorite of the dystopian lot is *Fahrenheit 451*, which shows what happens to the world when you take away books, the most powerful way to address and inspire consideration of important topics (though it also shows people seduced by pleasure and wall-to-wall reality shows).

What issues should you address? Can you lead your readers to consider weighty matters without spoiling the story? Can you leave them with a meaningful takeaway? Can you give your book this extra magical layer, the one that separates books quickly forgotten from ones that live forever?

Don't think meaningful books cannot also tell a rip-snorting good story. *Uncle Tom's Cabin* is basically a thriller. *A Christmas Carol* is a ghost story. *Pride and Prejudice* is a romance. The fact that you may be writing genre fiction does not mean it can't have value. To the contrary, you are far more likely to influence thought with a book that people read than with a book that no one reads. Maybe your story will be discovered and appreciated long after you're gone—but that's playing the long odds. Here's a better idea. Write a terrific story that rivets readers to the page—but also gives them something to think about when the story is finished.

Play for greater stakes. If you're going to take all the time and invest all the energy required to finish a book, why not make it the best book it possibly can be? Don't shy away from greatness because you're new to writing. More than once a famous writer's first book turns out to be their best. That's not always the case, but my point is, you should make every book—first, middle, or last—as strong and meaningful as it can possibly be. Don't sell your work short.

Aspire to greatness.

Highlights

1) Stories are the glue that binds us together and gives meaning to our fragile existence.

2) Readers are drawn to books that address issues that interest them or reinforce their preexisting beliefs.

3) Readers are drawn to books that fill needs or promise elusive wisdom.

4) Stories are inherently moral, and should help readers discover larger truths.

5) Theme should focus readers' attention on important questions —without attempting to force answers.

6) Great books address great themes.

Red Sneaker Exercises

1) If you haven't done it already, make a list of your three favorite books. (If you read *Story Structure*, maybe you'll remember what your three books were.) I know, you have far more than three favorites, but humor me and winnow it down to a short list that isn't too diffuse to analyze. Do you see a common theme emerging? Do your selections revolve around a central problem, idea, or concern? Do they take place in similar settings, or involve characters on similar journeys? Even if you can't quite fit all of them into the same pigeonhole, considering what made these books appeal to you should help you think about what you might like to do thematically with the book you're writing.

2) What news stories get your blood boiling? Many writers, from Thomas More to Ray Bradbury, have used fiction to point out society's ills or redirect society in a better direction. If you were to play Orwell or Huxley, what possible future would you caution readers about?

3) Historically, every era seems to have a dominant cause (at least in hindsight) that defines it. What do you think will be the defining issue of the time in which you live? This might be another approach to finding a theme to weave into your story. Current event themes seem to work best in mysteries or thrillers, while romances tend to lend themselves to more emotional themes, and science fiction often discusses the influence of technology on our future.

4) In *Excellent Editing*, I suggested that writers consider carrying a journal. I think all writers should have a means to jot down ideas so they don't lose them. Yes, I know you can dictate notes into your phone, and if that works for you, fine, though some of my best ideas come when I'm driving or in the shower or other places smartphones should not go. I know some people who don't keep journals or even refuse to make notes when ideas

occur to them, perhaps thinking that the act of writing an idea down will drain it of its potency. "If it was meant to be in the book, I'll remember it when the time comes." Well, that sounds romantic and artsy, but memory is fallible (increasingly so as age advances). I don't think I kill an idea by scribbling it down, but I do worry that great ideas might slip away because I didn't have a pencil at my fingertips.

3

FINDING YOUR THEME

"We write in ways that, we generally hope, reflect real life…. And in life, recurring themes are a recurring theme. We never quite conquer a pet vice or a relationship pattern or a communication habit. We're haunted by our particular demons."

— SARA ZARR

You may not know your theme when you start writing, and that's fine. As I've already indicated, you won't be the first. Theme can emerge in a later draft—just so long as it does eventually emerge. After you know where you're going, you can sharpen subsequent drafts to make the theme more consistent and as apparent as you want it to be.

Ideally, knowing your theme should help you make key decisions about your plot and your characters. It should inform decisions about what to cut and what not to cut. (Always try to write the first draft long—without unnecessary padding—so you can delete without worrying about word counts.) Cut what distracts from or contradicts the theme. Keep what reinforces it. Thomas Wolfe famously brought wagons filled with manuscript pages to his editor, Maxwell Perkins. Perkins pared this morass of words down to what pertained to a well-told story and the central theme as he perceived it, such as, for example, the fact that you can't go home again. This sharpening of focus was the difference between an unpublishable amateur effort and a tightly focused classic.

If you handle both the creation and the revision correctly, theme will add depth to your story. The repetition of thematic elements will create a meaningful resonance. This will enhance the reading experience for the attentive reader, and it won't hurt those who aren't (if you're telling an engaging story). In the next two chapters, we'll discuss how to find your theme and then, how to bring it to life in your work.

Unleash a theme that will give your story greater resonance.

FOLLOW YOUR PASSION

IN TODAY'S WORLD, THE PHRASE, "FOLLOW YOUR PASSION," HAS become a bit of a cliché, but as clichés go, it's a pretty darn good one. I will assume that you are passionate about books, stories, and writing, or you would not be reading this book. If you don't feel that passion, it's time to start thinking about a different way to spend your spare time. (I once encountered a young coed who said, "Mr. Bernhardt, I really want to be a writer, but I hate reading. What do you recommend?" I recommended a business degree.) There are likely a handful of subjects that attract you—or at the least, that you feel competent to write about. My first published novel, set in a law firm, was written when I worked full-time in a law firm. This shows either an intelligent attempt to put experience to use or a complete lack of imagination. You decide.

Often, a writer's interests become apparent in the course of a novel. Would it surprise you to learn that Dan Brown is fascinated by games, puzzles, conspiracies, art, history? I doubt it—his books are filled with all of the above. M.J. Rose's novels, starting with *The Reincarnationist*, present a world in which reincarnation is fact, not theory. Would it surprise you to learn that she is a passionate believer in past lives? Probably not. Or that Steve Berry is fascinated by history? Or that Ian Fleming once worked as a spy? My earliest books were set in the legal world, but they also advocated a point of view—a more positive view of lawyers and the legal system than was prevalent at the time. John Grisham's earliest books presented a more cynical view, sometimes equating lawyers to Mafiosi. Right or wrong, this worldview put him at the top of the charts.

Discover what you are passionate about.

Try to be as specific as possible. What matters to you? What's the message you would preach in your sermon on the mount? If you came down from Sinai with a bunch of tablets, what would be carved upon them?

Okay, let's try a more dramatic approach. Imagine that your nation has been overrun by an evil totalitarian government. You know, like the ones in dystopian YA novels. One day while you're at home working on your masterpiece, the government's thug-like minions, jackboots, stormtroopers (they all have them) burst into your writer garret. They've hacked your laptop, read your work, and decided that you are an enemy of the state. A person of interest. They burn your notes, erase your hard drive, lock you in a detainment center without trial, and go to work on your brain. Basically, they do what they did to Winston Smith in *1984*, except it doesn't work, because you're a writer, so you're smarter than the average bear. You persevere.

Twelve years later when you go to trial (represented by Ben Kincaid, I hope), you finally have a chance to speak.

What's your message?

If the judge gives you one minute, what will you say? If you get one page, what will you write? What is it the world needs to hear?

Maybe the radical underground sneaks a courier into a cell adjoining yours, but all you have is a scrap of paper. What will you send out into the world? What's your message in a bottle? What's your legacy? What do you want to be remembered for?

As God is my witness, I'll never be hungry again.

Tomorrow is another day.

I'm mad as hell and I'm not going to take it anymore.

Life is like a box of chocolates.

There's no place like home.

You may not think of those classic lines as themes—because a character actually says them—but they are. And they gave their stories resonance, gravitas, made them seem more important and more meaningful.

Let the story exemplify the theme that emerges from your passions.

Defiant Characters

Sometimes character can exemplify theme even better than plot. What characters have you chosen for your story? Will they help you say what you want to say?

In my writing retreats I ask people to think about who they admire most. Past or present, real or fictional, famous, infamous, or personal friend, it doesn't matter. Who is it? If you ask young people, they may identify a president, pop star, or actor, but people with more years under their belt may name a regular, non-famous person who made time for others, someone who didn't have to help and maybe couldn't afford to help, but nonetheless found a way to help. Who do you admire most?

Now ask yourself a follow-up question: Why?

What did they do? How did they live? What do they symbol-ize? What ideal do they represent in your mind?

How can you embody those same ideals in a character?

Not every character in your story has to be a saint. In fact, I think the fewer saints the better. I can't relate to perfect people. But while creating someone who is complex and flawed, can you nonetheless let them represent something greater? Maybe this is suggested by their mission statement, their goal or desire. Why do they want what they want? What does that tell you about them? Or maybe this is identified in a turning point they undergo during the story. In *Creating Character*, I discussed the concept of character arc. Protagonists are typically on a journey, from one end of a dichotomy to its polar opposite. How does that journey occur? When will the reader start to see it? What event signifies the change?

Is there a point when your character makes what amounts to a statement of purpose? Is there a point where the reader sees them becoming a different person?

If you want the theme to be the virtue of nonviolent change, then what real-life figures do you pattern your characters on? The guys who flew planes into the World Trade Center? No. The students at Tiananmen Square. The people who marched in Selma. Gandhi. In the Hunger Games trilogy, Katniss eventually becomes the leader of a movement for violent change. The final book has distressing consequences that some readers found almost too off-putting to bear—but for a reason. Suzanne Collins wasn't interested in a Disney ending. She wanted to make the point that violent revolution, no matter how well-intentioned, always leads to negative results, possibly more bad than good, even when "successful."

You need the right characters to represent the right theme.

Whether you are a fan of Ayn Rand's work or not, you have to admit that it has strong thematic content. The pro-business, pro-individualism message of *Atlas Shrugged* caused it to be embraced by a host of politicians, apparently unaware or unconcerned that the author was an atheist. To me, the scene in *The Fountainhead* when Howard Roark justifies destroying the building he designed is ludicrous. He's just cost his partners millions of dollars in a petulant violent act because he didn't get his way about everything. But to those who believe in Objectivism, or who believe artistic integrity is absolute, the scene is a meaningful evocation of an important principle.

Many classic novels involved characters who, due to circumstances outside their control, are placed in situations that force them to make difficult decisions. Moral choices. Forcing a character to fight their oppressors gives the writer an opportunity to rail against injustice. *The Scarlet Letter* (piety). *To Kill a Mockingbird* (bigotry). *Uncle Tom's Cabin* (slavery). *The Grapes of Wrath* (economic opportunism). *The Bonfire of the Vanities* (the "Me" Generation). *Ender's Game* (child abuse, racism, video games, war, etc.).

Put your characters in situations that make them realize what matters most—so readers can realize it too.

One of the best film comedies of the past half-century is *Groundhog Day*, which later found new life as a stage musical. Even if you haven't seen the film, you surely know the premise, since it's been stolen by countless television programs and movies ever since it was released. The idea is that a man finds himself repeatedly reliving the same day and is unable to stop it or move on. He eventually realizes that he's being given a chance to "get it right"—but what exactly does that mean? Those perceiving this as a rom-com might think he's being given a chance to win the affections of the lead female, who initially doesn't care for him at all. But midway through the film he manages to get her into bed—and nothing changes. The day restarts just as it did before.

Why? Because although he has changed the way someone else

perceives him, he himself has not changed at all. Both the plot
and the character arc are gently nudging us toward the larger
theme. He's not being given a chance to win the girl. He's being
given a chance to become an authentic, compassionate human
being. He starts the movie resentful, bitter, unhappy. But over the
course of reliving the same day for what must be at least five
years (judging from the piano skills he acquires), he gets over
himself, starts caring about others, and becomes a real person.
This being Hollywood, he does win the fair maiden, but not just
for a night. They initiate a real relationship, which is what a real
person deserves. The character's journey has been designed and
executed to exemplify the theme, a gentle message about the kind
of life we should all strive to achieve.

Many stories of injustice involve characters put into difficult
situations by the ways of the world, the society in which they
live. All are forced to do something to combat it. Sometimes they
are successful. Sometimes they are not. In fact, sometimes an
untraditional ending can give a theme more heft, more power.
But all of these ideas started with a writer who looked deep into
themselves. What's wrong with the world today? What do you
care about most? If you could change one thing, what would it
be? And then, after uncovering the answers, the authors looked
for ways to make those ideas come alive in their fiction.

Don't undersell your potential. Don't shy away from the difficult or the controversial. Let the story be about what you think
matters most. It's the surest way to create something worth reading, maybe for generations to come.

**Peer deeply into your heart and uncover the themes that
will distinguish your work.**

HIGHLIGHTS/EXERCISES

Highlights

1) Unleash a theme that will give your story greater resonance.

2) Discover what are you passionate about.

3) Let the story exemplify the theme that emerges from your passions.

4) You need the right characters to represent the right theme.

5) Put your characters in situations that make them realize what matters most—so readers can realize it too.

6) Peer deeply into your heart and uncover the themes that will distinguish your work.

Red Sneaker Exercises

1) When I wrote about finding themes that distinguish your

work, I intended "distinguish" to have both possible meanings. Theme should distinguish your book from others that may not be as strong in this department, and should also give it distinction, should make it a higher-caliber work. You have probably already made a conscious decision about the kind of story for which you would most like to be remembered. Now make the same decision in terms of theme. What do you want to represent in the minds of readers? What would you most like to be remembered for?

2) If you've been working your way through this series of books, then you've perhaps already outlined your work-in-progress and perhaps filled out some character detail sheets for your lead characters. Have you also given thought to character arc? What is your protagonist's journey? We all take hard knocks, but we are defined by how we deal with them. Are you suggesting there is always hope, always a chance to atone for past errors (a theme of universal appeal, for obvious reasons). Or are you suggesting the opposite theme? You may have already made some general choices, unintentionally, about theme.

3) If you haven't already done so, make a list of the three human beings you admire most. Just for this exercise, try to avoid fictional characters, politicians, or people who are famous for being famous. Focus on those you admire based upon their achievements. What is it that speaks to you so profoundly? Given the huge number of possibilities, they must have done something truly tremendous to merit their place on your list. What is it? You can admire a person for having the courage to take a stand without necessarily sharing their beliefs or admiring their cause. What should your protagonist represent? What makes this person unique? What makes them worthy of admiration—or the reader's time?

4) Take a look at your outline, specifically the challenges your protagonist will face on their journey to the climax. Have you chosen problems and obstacles that will exemplify the theme? Have you given them a chance to take stands that will bring the theme to life? In *Saving Private Ryan*, as Tom Hanks gasps his last breath, he tells the young solider he has saved, "Earn this." How have your protagonists earned the rewards they receive at the end of the story?

4

REVEALING YOUR THEME

"Literature must rest always on a principle, and temporal considerations are no principle at all...[N]o theme is inept, no past or present preferable."

— OSCAR WILDE

By now, I hope you're beginning to get a glimmer of what your core theme might be. Maybe it's not entirely fleshed out, but you've got a bit of a road map, a Google Maps diagram with an arrow pointing the right way. Now it's time to think about how to bring that theme to life in your work. As you may have guessed from what I've said in previous chapters, I think subtler is better, a feather brush is preferable to a sledge hammer, and if a few readers miss it altogether, so be it.

When I talk about people missing the point, what I'm really contemplating is the possibility of some readers missing that there *is* a point. The fact that different readers may interpret your book in differing ways is not necessarily a liability. Too much ambiguity can make a book seem vague and nebulous. This can lead readers to think it is muddled or not worth the trouble. But genuinely admitting multiple interpretations, all of them potentially valid, is the hallmark of great literature. Every reader comes to a book with a distinct past and personality, and that inevitably means they will read a work differently. This can lead to spirited debates, great book club meetings, and tenure-winning dissertations. I don't think you need to aim for full-out James Joyce enigmas. But why shouldn't a good book have just as much room for complexity and variation as life itself?

The best writing permits multiple interpretations. That enriches the narrative.

Question Me an Answer

First, let's make a distinction between the idea of thesis and the idea of theme. They are not the same thing. In fact, they are not even close. As you probably recall from high school English, a thesis should announce the central idea of your essay or argument. It should take a position rather than pose an inquiry, which is why teachers typically refer to it as a thesis *statement*. It should be as definite as possible, and everything in the paper should relate back to that thesis.

Theme is a completely different animal. If everything in your book directly relates back to your theme, you've probably written a parable or an allegory. If the story is in complete service to the theme, if you keep hitting people over the head with the theme (or symbols) constantly, no one will ever be immersed in the tale you're telling. Theme cannot and should not be as cut-and-dried as a thesis. And most importantly, the theme should pose a question, not deliver an answer. Get people thinking, but try to avoid telling them what to think.

Theme should ask a question, rather than insisting upon a particular answer.

John Gardner wrote about using theme to announce a topic for discussion, or to ask a question. Let's consider a story everyone knows: *Romeo and Juliet.* Is the theme Feuding Is Bad? Love Conquers All? I would say no to the last one (especially since the teen lovers never conquer much of anything), but others might disagree. Note how much more interesting the discussion becomes when you put the theme in the form of a question. Perhaps the theme is: Does Fighting Inevitably Destroy Innocents? Or Can Children Survive Their Parents? Can Love Survive Death?

When you think of it in terms of a question posed, as opposed to a message delivered, it changes your relationship to the story. After all, a question can be answered more than one way (and if it can't, the question is a waste of time). If the theme is Can Love Survive Death?, people with different perspectives, experiences, and personalities can answer in different ways that are still true to the story. The romantic can answer: Yes, even though the story ends tragically, the lovers find a way to make their love eternal. Or the political thinker can say: Yes, their end is tragic, but the strength of their love ultimately overcomes hate and ends the fighting. Or the cynical parent can say: They're stupid kids and they did something really stupid which is what happens when stupid kids don't get guidance and their stupid heads are filled with stupid romantic notions. Or hormones.

With this approach, the theme does not limit the work, but enriches it. Instead of writing yourself into a corner, you've written yourself into a great debate. You've given people something to think about, which will always be more stimulating than a sermon. Even though Shakespeare's play is capable of multiple interpretations, they all center around the idea of love, its centrality in our lives, and the tragedy of unfulfilled desire. This is what lends the play such enduring appeal. And theme can do the same for your work.

Theme should inspire people to think, not tell them what to think.

FINDING THE EMOTIONAL CORE

AS I MENTIONED, I'VE WRITTEN SEVERAL BOOKS THAT, ALTHOUGH I don't think they're particularly political, do address political issues. To put it a different way—I don't think the books take sides, but they are designed to inspire readers to think about the world in which they live and what they think it should look like. My characters have dealt with religion (*Criminal Intent*), racism (*Perfect Justice* and *Naked Justice*) environmental issues (*Dark Justice*), and terrorism (*Justice Returns*). And even though I studiously avoid preaching or telling readers what to think— there will always be those who believe I have. I've seen mail accusing me of being extreme left-wing and extreme right-wing, everything from a fascist to a socialist. Take it from me—no matter how careful you are, if your book has anything to say, there's someone out there who won't like it.

This is the bottom line: Ideas tend to divide us. Emotions, on the other hand, unite us. Emotions bring us together. We all share an emotional core. We have the same emotions and want the same emotional nurturance. We want to be loved, cherished, appreciated. We want strong families, happy children, prosperous neighbors. So for a writer, especially an early writer, it may be safer to make your reader *feel* the theme rather than think about it. An idea only expressed intellectually is a lecture. An idea wrapped inside an emotion will be more powerful, more penetrating, and as a result, more memorable. Anybody who has ever been inside a revival tent knows that preachers can talk and argue and quote scripture with little intellectual impact, but if they stir emotions, people run to the pulpit.

Express your theme by stirring emotions.

Let me give you an example. Earlier I mentioned my novel *Death Row*, which involved the death penalty. I knew this could be controversial, but I also thought my story needed to be told. This is our ultimate sanction, and we are virtually the only first-world nation that still employs it. Can we justify the executions in a system so flawed, so riddled with error?

What I just made was an intellectual argument—we make mistakes so we shouldn't be killing people. And that argument was never made in the course of this novel. Instead, I let the story center around Ben's client, Ray Goldman. Turns out Ben lost his case and as a result Ray is on death row. He's about to be executed when new evidence arises. Ben races against time to discover what happened before it's too late to save his client. My goal was not to give lectures or to make intellectual arguments about the wisdom of the death penalty. Instead, I tried to let the reader feel Ray's pain, to experience the horror of being behind bars for years, facing execution for a crime he insists he did not commit.

I guess I should give a spoiler alert here, because without revealing what happened or who was responsible, I will reveal that at the end of the book, Ray is free. Ben throws a little soiree back at his office to celebrate the man's release. Ray is calm and quiet, but he does notice the interaction between Ben and Christina, who at that point had been friends for a long time but never anything more. And at some point, Ray just can't keep quiet.

"You know," he says, "if I learned anything from my seven years behind bars, it's this—every day is precious. You can't waste a single minute."

Ben gets the message. For the first time, he asks Christina out.

And the book implicitly captures its theme, without lecturing or polemicizing. Life is precious. Every single day. We can't afford to waste a minute.

And we can't afford to waste our reader's time, either.

SIGNS AND SYMBOLS

REMEMBER THAT ENGLISH TEACHER WHO TRIED TO HAMMER HOME concretized messages about theme by pointing to symbols? Sometimes symbols do suggest the author's theme. The problem I always had with this is that the reasoning seems circular. How do you recognize what is and is not a symbol? By understanding the theme. How do you understand the theme? By looking for symbols. In other words, there's a serious chicken-and-the-egg problem.

That said, once you've found the emotional core of your theme, symbolism might provide a subtle way of indicating it without expressing it in overt pronouncements. I don't know what kind of story you're writing, but I don't need psychic powers to realize that it probably involves some physical objects. I would even go so far as to suggest that there may be recurring physical objects that attract a certain degree of attention.

Could those physical objects be some sort of symbol? And if so, what exactly would they symbolize? You could conceivably pack a lot of meaning in a powerful package, without slowing or interrupting the story in the slightest.

A powerful symbol can reveal the theme.

Let's consider a few examples. Have you read *The Lord of the Rings*? Odds are you have. And what's the most dominant symbol in this epic saga? The rings, of course. In particular, the one ring to rule them all. And what does that ring symbolize? Power. The whole epic saga is a consideration of power and its use, for good or ill. Sauron wants power to dominate others. Gandalf marshals his powerful fellowship to ensure that power rests with those worthy of it. He specifically wants to destroy the ring, an instrument of such power that no one can be trusted to use it wisely. As Lord Acton told us years before, "Absolute power corrupts absolutely." So the ring must be consigned to the fires of Mordor. These were serious issues in Tolkien's era, just after WWII, and they are the core of this beloved fantasy classic.

Let's switch to one of my family's favorite movies, *The Incredibles*. This was such a hit with my children that we saw it three consecutive weekends. Each time the kids left yammering about how much cooler we would be if we had superpowers. What would our powers be? Obviously that movie touched something profound, even in a young audience. Which of course inspired me to think about what that might be.

This film involves a nuclear family, a structure everyone can relate to, and gives each member special abilities that are not chosen at random but are closely related to—one might say, are symbolic of—their personalities.

For instance, the father, the man carrying the world on his shoulders, gets super strength (and when powers are outlawed, he is unhappy, emasculated, and working at a boring desk job). The mother, always juggling chores and tugged in a dozen different directions at once, has elastic stretching powers. She needs them. The insecure, unpopular teenage girl with body-image issues has the power of invisibility. What teenager ever didn't wish she could just disappear? She can also project a force field—a sure way of keeping others at a distance. And the hyperactive OCD preteen is the speedster, always on the move, never in one place for long. All the tensions that comprise an American family are encapsulated in this group—and their powers symbolically indicate their individual issues. Only Mrs. Incredible, with her infinitely stretching arms, could hold this family together.

Symbols can be preachy and obvious, but I would urge you not to do that. Don't be so insecure about readers "getting it" that you end up doing something boring. It might make more of an impact if readers have to work for it a bit, if they get that magical epiphany, the "aha" moment. *Eureka! I've figured this out!* It will stick with readers much longer. In fact, I would avoid any instances of inserting a symbol just for the sake of having a symbol. Instead of artificially implanting something that doesn't have to be there, use what's already in the story for a reason. Just find ways to make more of it.

Turn the objects already in the story into your symbols, rather than imposing unneeded objects just for the sake of having symbols.

In Larry McMurtry's *The Last Picture Show* (or the fine Bogdonavich film adaptation), the highly symbolic title has not been chosen by accident. It points toward a larger theme. After all, this book isn't actually about movies. The last picture show— the closing of the local theater—is emblematic of a dying Texas town, and that in itself is emblematic of McMurtry's true subject —the passing of a way of life. Small towns, like small town theaters, are being erased, replaced by larger entities, corporations, theater chains, and an inherent loss of simplicity and innocence. In Ray Bradbury's *The Incredible Ice Cream Suit*, a single nice set of clothes shared by many lower-income men represents a better way of life, something they can only fantasize about—or pretend to have one day a week, when the suit is theirs. Ken Follett titled his epic work of British history *The Pillars of the Earth*, a reference to the cathedral that is the center of the novel just as it becomes the center of the lives of the many souls chronicled in the narrative.

By now, you should be getting a sense of what your core theme might be, and better yet, its emotional center. Now you can think about how to represent that theme, how to stir those emotions in your narrative—without impairing or interrupting your story. What will your symbols be? How will you deploy them? Once you integrate these elements into your tale, you are on the path to telling a story that's not only a page-turner, but might touch readers in a meaningful way.

Are there ways to make it even better? Can you use theme to create resonance that makes the book even more powerful? I think you can.

HIGHLIGHTS/EXERCISES

Highlights

1) The best writing permits multiple interpretations. That enriches the narrative.

2) Theme should ask a question, rather than insisting upon a particular answer.

3) Theme should inspire people to think, not tell them what to think.

4) Express your theme by stirring emotions.

5) A powerful symbol can reveal the theme.

6) Turn the objects already in the story into your symbols, rather than imposing unneeded objects just for the sake of having symbols.

Red Sneaker Exercises

1) Try a different approach to theme. Instead of trying to seize an idea, see if you can capture an emotion. Pick an emotion that's relevant to the book you're writing, then see if you can develop its corresponding idea. For instance, if your theme is injustice, perhaps the corresponding emotion is anger, or jealousy, or revenge. If you're writing a coming of age story, perhaps the corresponding emotion is curiosity, or insecurity. Frame your theme in terms of emotions rather than ideas and see if you can invest the story with something much more elemental—and potent.

2) In the film world, Alfred Hitchcock used the term "McGuffin" to describe the elusive object that all the characters want. It might be a secret, a document, a piece of microfilm, a valuable diamond, etc. The point of the somewhat derisive term "McGuffin" is that, at least to Hitchcock, it didn't much matter what it was. You just needed something to motivate the characters to chase one another.

What are the McGuffins in your story? If you're writing a mystery or thriller, there must be something the characters want or want to know. In a SF or fantasy epic, do they all want a ring, a force, a weapon, or a power? In women's fiction, what does the protagonist need to make her life seem fulfilled? And now that you've identified the McGuffins—can you use them as symbols? Can you choose one of several possible McGuffins because it is the best symbol to represent your theme? The thematic quality will be stronger if you use something that's in the story for a reason, rather than introducing something (say, Forest Gump's floating feather) that plays no part in the story and is only there for symbolic reasons.

3) In high school or college debate programs, participants are asked to argue a "resolution," which is basically a question that both sides are going to address. I don't think you should turn

your story into a debate, but if you were going to, what would be the central resolution? What is the core thematic idea all the characters are dancing around? What are the differing sides, the pros and cons? How can they best be represented in your story? Try to avoid reducing it to something like, good guys have good ideas, bad guys have bad ideas. You might produce a more intriguing book if your characters go somewhere unexpected (which is why at the outset of *Capitol Conspiracy*, long-time bleeding heart Ben Kincaid stuns his friends by taking an extremely conservative position—moved by a terrorist attack that has left his best friend in critical condition).

5

CREATING RESONANCE

"Ultimately, your theme will find you. You don't have to go looking for it."

— RICHARD RUSSO

In the previous chapter I considered how to reveal your theme. Now I will address how to create resonance, how to cause that theme to suffuse the story in a way that is simultaneously powerful yet unforced.

If you've been writing long, you've probably heard or read the expression "Show, don't tell." This is one of the most frequently quoted writing aphorisms—and also one of the least well understood. A woman in the audience at a writing conference once called me on this. She said, "Look, when you're writing a book, sometimes you've just gotta tell. Otherwise, no one will know what's going on." And you know what? She's right. When it comes to defining the plot, moving the story forward, describing the action, sometimes you've just gotta tell.

When writers talk about showing, it's not usually in regard to plot, but character. In this respect, character is much like theme.

The information you give the reader will have more impact when you suggest rather than hammer. Details you force-feed the reader tend not to stick. On the other hand, when you suggest or imply, forcing readers to do some of the work themselves, it has more impact.

Here's what you need to understand: As soon as you describe the character's function—teacher, preacher, lawyer, stalker, guy with a gun—readers have already conjured a mental image based upon their previous experiences with life and stories. There's not much you can do to prevent that. Dumping a lot of physical description about hair color, height, eyes, etc., probably won't stick. You'll have more impact if you stop trying to change what readers already have and instead try to provide the details they haven't supplied yet. Instead of telling them what the person looks like, tell them who the person is. Give the reader insight into your character's inner life, their personality, their core—not by telling them about it, but by showing it in action.

Showing is particularly important when it comes to describing emotional states. As discussed in the previous chapter, emotion binds us together, and when you connect readers to a character emotionally, they are far more likely to care about and be invested in the plot. So avoid telling statements such as, "He felt exasperated" or "She was furious." Instead, *show* the reader what's going on in your character's head. "She ran up the stairs, slammed the door, threw herself on the bed, pounded the pillows, and wept." Okay, that's a bit over the top, but can you see the difference? Showing paints a far more powerful portrait than telling.

When conveying theme, show, don't tell.

Conveying theme works exactly the same way. Avoid anything heavy-handed or obvious. Theme should be the sweetening in the tea, not the tea itself. Books written for the sole purpose of getting some message across rarely succeed. So never announce your theme in the text, or make it explicit in the epigram, or put it in boldface type, or have an elderly sage deliver it on the final page. That approach is more likely to turn people off than to indoctrinate or inculcate. Grownups like to be treated like grownups, not lectured to like children. You're not writing Aesop's fables. You're writing a novel you want to be taken seriously, with a theme you want to give it the extra weight needed to make it truly special.

Reveal your theme in action.

Don't deliver the theme—dramatize it. Make the reader feel the theme instead of telling it. Reveal your deepest beliefs about human beings. Show characters pursuing paths that illustrate what you're talking about. Is this the best way to live a life? Is there a better approach? Why is one superior to another?

Most classic books and films illustrate some major theme. Of the five "plots," or character arcs discussed in *Perfecting Plot*, by far the most popular are the education plot and the redemption plot—because they both tend to illustrate people seeking better, richer lives, a quest that most readers find appealing. One of my favorite films, *Casablanca*, is about Rick Blaine, who starts the film bruised and disillusioned, hiding behind a tough-guy veneer, but at the end makes a tremendous sacrifice and joins a nobler cause.

Another popular film, *E.T.*, is ostensibly a children's SF film, but at its core is a meditation on friendship. At the start of the film, Elliott has no friends. Then he gets one (from outer space). This friendship gives Elliott strength and helps him overcome his insecurities. And when it's time for his friend to go home, he learns what we all do when we grow up—that friendship has a cutting edge. Sometimes, we have to say goodbye.

The Terminator and *Jurassic Park* (and many other SF films) are cautionary tales about the threat posed by technology advancing more quickly than our emotional maturity. *Thelma and Louise* was about the oppression of women by men—another topic we are still not dealing with adequately. But you will never find any place in these films where the themes are announced as such. Instead, they make you love the characters, draw you into the conflict—then let the theme emerge on its own terms.

Effective Subplotting

In the previous chapter, I discussed using symbols to indicate theme. Another way to get there—without announcing it in so many words—is through subplots. Too often, writers use subplots to complicate (or lengthen) the story. I want my characters to be more complex, so let me add a personal trauma. Or I'm afraid the story drags, so let me add a sex scene (requiring a partner, a shower, etc.). Subplots should deepen the characters and the tale. But you can also use subplots to heighten the theme in ways that aren't telling but will be perceived by most readers.

Subplots can emphasize theme.

The father figures in all the various subplots of *Cruel Justice* helped reinforce the theme. John Mortimer used essentially the same approach in his Rumpole stories. The main plot and subplots were thematic mirrors of one another. For that matter, the same linkage appears in almost every episode of *Rick and Morty*. The SF story involving the title characters is connected thematically to the domestic story involving the parents or sister. Can you do this in your story? Once you've recognized what the central theme might be, it will be easier to create parallels in your subplots without doing anything forced or unnatural. Subplots should relate back to the main plot in some way. This is an extension of the same idea. In addition to relating to the plot, the subplots will also relate to the central theme.

Let me use another great film as an example: *Tootsie*. This is a terrific comedy that, given the depth of its exploration of gender identity issues, was well ahead of its time. The movie revels in its gender roles, gender stereotypes, gender confusion—all working together to reinforce the central theme. As you may recall, the actor played by Dustin Hoffman disguises himself as a woman to get work on a soap opera. Ultimately, he discovers that being a woman has made him a better man. But there's much more than that happening. He has a girlfriend, played by Teri Garr, and becoming a woman helps him understand why he has been such a poor boyfriend. He develops a relationship with Jessica Lange— who only likes him as a woman. Her father wants to marry him. The soap's leading man wants to seduce him. And he has to deal with sexual harassment from a director. None of these subplots was chosen by accident. All draw attention to the central thematic questions. What does it mean to be a man? What does it mean to be a woman?

THE LIGHT AND THE DARK

I URGE YOU TO RESIST THE TEMPTATION TO EMBODY THE CORRECT approach to life, the one advocated by your theme, in the "good guy," while revealing the antithesis in the "bad guy." That's too obvious and you can do better. In the first place, in previous books I've advised you to avoid anything so obvious as a "bad guy." Your protagonist should have opposition, but it should be motivated in a believable way, something deeper than, "They're evil," or "They're greedy" or anything so simplistic. Conflict is sharper when the villains have strong, credible reasons for doing what they do. Similarly, I would urge you to avoid having them embody simplistic viewpoints or worldviews that no one in the real world actually has, just to make some thematic point.

Now we come to the big "however." I do believe there are circumstances in which it is viable to have the protagonist and antagonist embody opposing viewpoints. Just don't make it so black and white, so polarized, that the conflict becomes infantile. Many children's films employ obvious good guy-bad guy tropes —and that's why they remain children's films. Action-adventure stories too often rely on absurdly evil villains to give their heroes someone appalling to fight. (Why would anyone want to rule the world anyway? Sounds like a lot of thankless work to me.) I feel the same way about antagonists who want to make more money than they could possibly spend or get revenge against people who will never know what happened. Even beloved films like *Star Wars* are essentially good guy-bad guy (Rebels-Empire) dichotomies. In the original trilogy, there's little exploration of what's wrong with the Empire—but Darth Vader wears black, and he's mean, so the Empire must be destroyed. We are given some quasi-spiritual business about "using the force" which suggests that the Rebel path has an inherent goodness—though what exactly that might be is never explained or explored.

The protagonist and antagonist are on different journeys— and those differences could relate to the theme.

You may be able to use your antagonist to reveal the dark side (yes, I really said that) of your theme. If the protagonist's journey reveals a path to the light, the antagonist's journey can reveal an alternate route. But make sure those journeys mean something. One path isn't automatically better simply because that's what the protagonist is doing. It should represent something desirable, something inherently better. Readers may not automatically agree with your depiction of what's good and what's not. But if you dramatize it effectively, you might cause your readers to give it some thought.

Consider Ken Kesey's brilliant book, *One Flew Over the Cuckoo's Nest* (adapted into a fine Milos Forman film). McMurphy gets himself committed to a mental institution, thinking this will be a softer way to work off his sentence than prison. But while there, he encounters Nurse Ratched, a domineering control freak who does not appreciate his iconoclastic rule-breaking attitude. This is a fairly simple dichotomy. McMurphy represents the freedom of the human spirit. Ratched represents the repression of the human spirit. But it's not quite that cut and dried. McMurphy (and his disciples) seem to be analogized to another famous iconoclast—Jesus of Nazareth. But he's also a criminal—which suggests rule-breaking taken too far, so far it harms others. Ratched is controlling, but at the same time, she has a difficult job and is struggling as best she can to maintain order (the excuse used by every fascist since the dawn of time). The dichotomy is there, but it's far from simplistic or black-and white.

Even popular films can be surprisingly complex in their portrayal of characters and the complexity of the themes they are allowed to embody. The early Sean Connery James Bond films were popular, but that Bond was far from a white hat or goody-two-shoes (which was part of his appeal). His insouciant callousness was a stark contrast to most superheroes. His womanizing was equally hard to admire. In two of the films, he swivels a woman around to take a bullet for him. Not exactly a Superman move. In these films, the good guy is in many respects not far removed from the bad guys.

By presenting both sides of a thematic issue, you may suggest that they are not so different.

In *Raiders of the Lost Ark*, the first Indiana Jones picture, Indy is presented as a college professor and archeologist who travels the world in search of artifacts for the college museum—and to save the world from destruction. The ostensible villain, Belloq, is also an archeologist, but one who has fallen in league with the Nazis. Indy considers himself the good guy in this story, but Belloq has a different view. "You and I are very much alike. Archeology is our religion. Yet we have both fallen from the pure faith." He notes that neither of them is a conventional archaeologist, and Indy's methods are no more scientifically approved than his.

Belloq suggests that he is a "shadowy reflection" of Indy. One bad break would be enough to turn Indy into Belloq, to "push you out of the light." These are not simply random words. Indeed, this distinction turns out to be crucial. In the climactic scene, when Belloq opens the Lost Ark and the—whatever they are—are released, Indy refuses to look. That's what saves him. But Belloq believes the blinding light is beautiful, so he looks. And becomes a puddle on the floor. The fundamental differences between them, the principles their differing journeys embody, have led to drastically different results—creating a stark thematic contrast.

Play Fair with Your Opponents

THERE IS ALWAYS A TENDENCY TO PRESENT OUR PROTAGONISTS IN an aggrandizing, heroic light—and to do exactly the opposite with the antagonists. Resist this temptation. Yes, you want your readers to like the protagonist, but there's nothing wrong with having them like the bad guy a bit too. Many stories have succeeded based upon the likeability of villains and rogues, like Hannibal Lector, J.R. Ewing, Mr. Ripley, to name a few. There is nothing wrong with this. Readers may be a trifle sad when charming villains are defeated, but they wouldn't have it any other way. Heroes are more interesting when they are flawed, and villains are better when they are not ridiculously vile.

If these opposing forces represent opposing sides of your thematic question, that should also be presented in a less simplistic manner. Or to put it differently: Don't overtly play favorites. Present the opposing force with just as much power and fairness. Be an equal opportunity writer. It's easy to fall into the trap of being so passionate about what you're trying to say that you end up being one-sided or dogmatic. No one was ever persuaded by a one-sided argument. To the contrary, that approach gives opponents an opportunity to say, Well, he didn't even mention this case, or that exception, or another side's argument. This is deadly. This is when your theme turns into a sermon—worse, a biased, one-sided sermon. This is when your viewpoint becomes a screed. No one will be converted. No one will be convinced.

Present both sides of your thematic question with equal vigor.

The remedy? Make sure both sides are represented fairly. Like Gardner said—Don't take sides, present the question. Back both with supportive arguments. Let the reader decide. If you've structured this properly, you will lead readers where you want them to go, but it won't seem so obvious and argumentative that they resist the journey.

Any time you can convey a thematic question with multiple possible answers, none of which is necessarily wrong, you will have a powerful drama. The best part of the excellent film, *Kramer vs. Kramer*, is the trial. For most of the movie, we've sympathized with the father (Dustin Hoffman again). Only natural. We watched his wife walk out on her husband and child, and we have observed his struggle to become a more attentive parent. But at the trial, we get both sides. Sure, we continue to sympathize with the father, but we also see that the mother (Meryl Streep) has a valid position. Truth is, her husband was self-absorbed and little help around the house. Isn't she entitled to have a life too?

In another great film, *Unforgiven*, Clint Eastwood plays a former gunslinger dragged into a conflict between prostitutes seeking revenge and local law enforcement. He's only involved because he needs money to support his kids. He has no grudge against anyone nor any desire to return to his former violent ways. But after his friend is captured and killed, he's forced to become the gunslinger again. Gene Hackman, the sheriff, says, "You can't kill me. I'm building a house!" He's making a valid point. He's not a criminal or a bad guy, just a man doing the best he can with a poor situation. There is no right or wrong here—just two different approaches, two different views of the universe.

This film is particularly brave because it calls into question all those previous Eastwood films in which he played the loner Man With No Name who rides into town and sets things right with his guns. Was that character really a good guy? Or just a violent fascist with a talent for getting his way? Because Eastwood doesn't back away from a complex argument, because he presents both sides of the question with equal force, the film became more than yet another Western. It became a Best Picture winner and an enduring classic people still discuss and debate.

Give your book a chance to obtain the same status.

Give both sides a fair shot.

Use Your Words

ONE LAST SUGGESTION FOR PRESENTING YOUR THEME—WEAVE IT into the dialogue. If there's been a consistent refrain in all the books in this series, it is surely this: dialogue is your friend. Readers like dialogue. It quickens the pace and deepens the engagement. It is infinitely variable and can be used for a variety of purposes. In *Creating Character*, I discussed how to use dialogue to enrich characterization. In *Story Structure*, I discussed how to use dialogue to create story beats. In *Dynamic Dialogue*, I discussed all of the above and much more. Now let's consider how to use dialogue to deepen your theme.

Most importantly, avoid being direct. No one wants a character who announces the theme, not even in interior monologue. If it's spelled out for the reader, it won't have much impact. Leave the readers room to do some work themselves. But clever, well-considered dialogue can guide them where you want them to be. Off-the-nose dialogue is best—that is, dialogue in which characters aren't saying what's foremost in their minds. Have your characters talk around the subject, inevitably leading readers to wonder, What's going on here? In this way, off-the-nose dialogue can help your reader discover what lies beneath the surface.

Use dialogue to point readers toward your theme.

I mentioned *Casablanca*, a great film with some of the best dialogue ever written. There's an early moment when Rick, encouraged to do something noble, says, "I stick my neck out for nobody." Grammar concerns aside, this is a great line Bogie delivers like the seasoned actor he was. On one level, it's just Rick's way of saying no. But on a deeper level, it represents his isolationist position. He's not getting involved in the burgeoning worldwide conflict, the Nazi occupation of France, or anything else. This could be seen as the selfish view of a man who has been burned by love, but on a much larger level, it represents the isolationist position advocated by many in the USA.

Many people at the time objected to the US involvement in the "conflict overseas." We got dragged into a world war once before, they said. Let's be smarter this time. Rick starts that way, but over the course of the film, Ilsa Lund and Victor Laszlo prove that he cannot remain neutral. Indeed, they show him that neutrality is immoral and tantamount to aiding the Nazis. By the end of the film, Rick has become a freedom fighter, walking off with Claude Rains, "La Marseillaise" piping in the background, to join the Resistance. I suspect there were few in the audience in the 1940s who were not moved by his conversion.

A completely different but equally memorable film, *Sunset Boulevard*, involves the former silent picture star, Norma Desmond, discovered by a small-time scriptwriter, Joe Gillis. This is another film with memorable dialogue that provides insight into the characters and the theme. "I'm ready for my close-up," indicates Norma's dangerous insanity and self-delusion in a way sure to send chill bumps up the spine. Earlier in the film, when Joe first recognizes her, he says, "You're Norma Desmond. You used to be in silent pictures. You used to be big." Norma famously replies, "I am big. It's the pictures that got small." This is a neon sign pointing to the theme. Using Gardner's definition, the theme or topic here is fame (or perhaps, success). Is it really something to strive for, something desirable? Or is it simply narcissism and greed? Does it have any intrinsic worth, or is it a sign of spiritual emptiness?

Can you use dialogue, or any of the other tools discussed in this chapter, to indicate theme, to make it more powerful, more penetrating? If you do it well enough, it could have tremendous ripples. You could use these tools to tie your story into universal themes of enormous appeal.

HIGHLIGHTS/EXERCISES

Highlights

1) When conveying theme, show, don't tell.

2) Reveal your theme in action.

3) Subplots can emphasize theme.

4) The protagonist and antagonist are on different journeys—and those differences could relate to the theme.

5) By presenting both sides of a thematic issue, you may suggest that they are not so different.

6) Present both sides of your thematic question with equal vigor.

7) Use dialogue to point readers toward your theme.

Red Sneaker Exercises

1) Look at that outline and see if you can find opportunities to show your theme in action. Could the conflict be presented differently? Could the antagonist's motivation change? Should your hero have a different approach to problem-solving, or different obstacles on the journey? If you consider these plot and character points in terms of theme, you may find ways of deepening and improving your story.

2) Make a list of the subplots in your story. Even if this is a full-length novel, there should be fewer than ten, probably around five (if you have more, your book may be too busy, or may suffer from unclear goals or story question). Your subplots may involve a love interest, a family relationship, a job opportunity, an internal conflict, or a psychological problem. Do these subplots emphasize the theme? If not, could you tweak them so they do?

3) What kind of plot are you writing? Is your hero on a quest for redemption, or knowledge, or maturity? Is the hero being tested? Are they headed for disillusionment or corruption? In broad strokes, outline the progress of the journey. Now do the same for the antagonist. Do these journeys represent two sides of the same theme? Do they reflect the positive and the negative, or perhaps, the ambiguity between the two? If not, how could you adjust these journeys so they better reflect the ideas you want to put into play?

4) Consider your use of dialogue. Are you using it to maximum benefit? Does it quicken the pace of your scenes? And when characters speak to one another, is the dialogue on-the-nose or off-the-nose? When it's off-the-nose, what are they *not* talking about? What's the elephant in the room, the secret subject no one will directly address? Does that indicate a theme? Do the different approaches or positions of the characters illustrate that theme?

5) In one boldface sentence, write down your theme. Got it? Now I want you to make sure none of your characters ever says that, or anything like that. You don't want to be so obvious. But how can you bring that theme to light without ever having it spoken aloud?

6

UNIVERSAL THEMES

"If a theme or idea is too near the surface, the novel becomes simply a tract illustrating an idea."

— ELIZABETH BOWEN

Sometimes aspiring writers will ask: Should I write on one of the great themes, the subjects artists have addressed since the dawn of time? Or should I try to write about something new?

This is a toughie, in part because the answer hinges upon your definition of theme. Perhaps we should introduce new terminology: macro-theme and micro-theme. The micro-theme, in my mind, is closer to what Gardner was talking about—a topic for consideration. This is smaller and more specific, and consequently, it may be possible to find a new one. But on a larger level, that micro-theme probably relates to a universal theme.

Let me give you an example. *Capitol Conspiracy*, as I mentioned before, was spurred by the Patriot Act. That was a new piece of legislation, so that particular idea may not have appeared much in fiction. But the larger theme, the conflict between security and idealism, between the historic American devotion to human rights and the inherent desire for safety, was not new. Both FDR and Lincoln circumscribed human rights in treacherous times. So while the micro-theme may have been new, the larger idea was anything but.

Ideally, you want to address both a macro-theme and a micro-theme. (I know, just when you thought you had this thing figured out.) One may be a tool for reaching the other. This presents writers with a chicken and the egg problem. Should you start with a plot about the micro-theme, then try to uncover the macro-theme to which it relates? Or should you start with the larger, more universal idea, then determine how to address it in your story?

There is no certain answer. It ultimately goes back to why you write. What are you hoping to accomplish? I usually devise the story first, something I want to write about, and let the theme emerge later. You may have a burning desire to address a theme and need a plot to get there. Either approach works. Just make sure you instill both the micro-theme and the macro-theme in your story.

The micro-theme is a specific topic for consideration. The macro-theme is a universal theme that relates to the human condition.

THROUGH THE UNIVERSAL

OFTEN WHEN PEOPLE DISCUSS THEME THEY TALK IN TERMS OF dichotomies, opposing forces or ideas. Man vs. Nature, or Nature vs. Nurture. The Individual vs. the State. Good vs. Evil. (Has any book advocated the superiority of evil?) Man vs. Woman. Altruism vs. Self-Interest. And so forth. *One Flew Over the Cuck-oo's Nest* discusses freedom vs. control, or put in political terms, anarchy vs. order. *Casablanca* discusses separation vs. reunion, or perhaps, narcissism vs. socialization. All the dystopian classics — *1984, Brave New World, Fahrenheit 451*, are variations on the theme of personal expression and collective security. But are there some over-arching, or universal, themes?

In *Perfecting Plot*, I reduced character arcs to five repeating patterns (and I've yet to see anyone suggest a single story that did fit into one of the five patterns). Similarly, I will suggest that all themes, at the larger, macro-theme level, fit into one of three categories.

All themes fall into one of three universal categories, the conflicts between: 1) survival vs. extinction, 2) separation vs. reunion, and 3) isolation vs. socialization.

Of course, as you've probably already recognized, all these macro-themes are so large I can cram a lot of material into them. At the same time, I think each speaks to something real, an inherent longing within the human spirit, and this may be why they have appeared so often in fiction and work so well in stories. They speak to us in ways that all readers understand. They touch upon something hard-wired into the human identity.

Survival vs. Extinction

I listed this theme first because it has appeared so frequently in recent years. Dystopian novels have found tremendous popularity, especially—and this is important—among young adult readers. There are probably sound sociological reasons, especially given what seems like an alarming increase in terrorism and domestic violence. Fortunately, we don't have to determine why this is happening. We observe that it is, and consequently, readers may well be interested in books addressing the theme.

I've phrased this theme broadly for a reason. This should encompass far more than dystopian SF. A wide range of stories touch upon this fundamental dichotomy. Any story addressing injustice, equal rights, prejudice, or economic inequality, fits within the category. It doesn't have to be about the survival of the species. It could be about the survival of a discrete group of people—a race, creed, or color—or it could be about the survival of a family, or even a particular individual.

Survival themes may address the continued existence of the species, a discrete group, or even an individual.

Stories about forms of prejudice can be enormously powerful, and indeed, writers employing this theme have frequently been at the forefront of the movement for change. I've mentioned the impact of *Uncle Tom's Cabin*. In more recent years, we've seen similar themes discussed in books like *To Kill a Mockingbird*, *The Color Purple*, or *The Help*. Prejudice not only divides us, but threatens the autonomy or survival of a distinct class of people.

Prejudice, however, is not the only problem that divides us, or that threatens human survival. Some believe technology, computers, and the increasing abilities of AI, pose a powerful threat to our continued existence. Chaplin, being the genius he was, saw this coming from a distance, and made it the theme of *Modern Times*. *Brave New World* considered the impact of pharmaceuticals—more relevant today than it was when Huxley wrote the book. Any number of SF novels have addressed the threats posed by robots, androids, and artificial intelligence.

I would put war stories in this category as well, and there have been many of them, understandably, since there have been many wars, and there seems to be no foreseeable end to them any time soon. *All Quiet on the Western Front. Catch-22. Slaughterhouse-Five. The Forever War.* In a slight variation on this theme, sometimes the opposition is not a foreign government but some other equally powerful organization, as in *Three Days of the Condor* (based upon the apparently lengthier book, *Six Days of the*

Condor). The villain turns out to be not a foreign government but an organization within our own government—the CIA. In *The Da Vinci Code*, the threat is posed by the Church and religious organizations such as the Priory of Sion and Opus Dei, which are longer-lived and broader-based than any single government.

I would also put legal thrillers in this category. More often than not, they involve an innocent man—or one who might be innocent—fighting government forces for survival. Like my Ben Kincaid novels. Erle Stanley Gardner's Perry Mason books, which are still the bestselling series of all time. Television programs such as *The Fugitive*. And on a more existential level, Kafka's *The Trial*. In *The Shawshank Redemption* (based upon a Stephen King novella), it's the justice and penal systems that threaten continued survival.

Finally, I will suggest that this macro-theme also includes smaller, more personal stories in which an individual's survival is threatened, in effect, by themselves, or the dark forces lurking within them. These have also seen a dramatic increase in recent years, and based upon what I've seen at my retreats, there's a decent chance this is what you're writing. This would include stories of corruption such as *The Treasure of the Sierra Madre*. *Macbeth*. *Citizen Kane*. *Wall Street*. *All the King's Men*. Whether it's money, gold, political capital, quiet influence, or unbridled power, the corrupting force inevitably leads to personal destruction. Sexual desire can be equally destructive, something Vladimir Nabokov made clear decades ago in *Lolita*, Margaret Mitchell demonstrated in *Gone With the Wind*, and filmmakers addressed more recently in *Fatal Attraction*, *Rambling Rose*, and *American Beauty*. For that matter, characters with self-destructive tendencies often appear in crime and mystery fiction.

SEPARATION VS. REUNION

.   .   .

As many scribes have noted, we are born alone and die alone. Is it any wonder then, that we spend so much time in between searching for companionship? This goes far beyond boy-meets-girl stories. This pertains to all the different ways people can become isolated, alienated, segregated, or alone. There are many ways this can happen. You may first notice it in school, when you're either in the cool group or on the outside scorning the cool group (probably the latter, since you're a writer). People have a natural longing for companionship, for support, for security, for home. This speaks to our most primal, most essential needs—intimacy, warmth, safety, acceptance.

This is probably also the reason for the enormous popularity of the "redemption plot," in which characters who have erred, sinned, or fallen from grace manage to redeem themselves. Truth is, we've all screwed up, probably more than once. We may accept responsibility for our errors or we may not, but either way, we hope to somehow, some way, compensate for them. Ultimately, these stories are about hope, which may be elusive, may even be unobtainable. But we would all like to believe that hope is out there somewhere, which is undoubtedly why this macro-theme has such appeal. It leaves the reader with hope for a better tomorrow, regardless of what happened in the past.

The longing for connection and meaning is the source of endless thematic material.

The Verdict by Barry Reed, was on the surface a legal thriller, but also a character-driven drama about a lawyer fallen from grace—fallen apart, really—and hoping that one last case might be enough to give his life value. Many current thrillers have heroes with tortured or troubled pasts, and their heroic exploits are a means of clawing out of the abyss. Lee Child's enormously popular Jack Reacher character is a former major in the Army Police Corps who, due to events revealed piecemeal throughout the series, leaves the service to wander the world, stopping frequently to help those deserving his assistance. Clint Eastwood's thriller *In the Line of Fire* features a Secret Service agent who failed to prevent the assassination of JFK, and thus is determined not to fail the current president—even though he thinks the man is kind of a jerk.

This macro-theme also encompasses underdog stories, and there have been many of those, both in film and fiction. To paraphrase John Grisham, Americans love underdogs. We love to watch the little guy rise—until he becomes too successful—then we love to watch him fall. There is, sadly, some truth in that. Writers can tell the story on either side of the apex—the rise or the fall—or both. Every summer there's a new sleeper cinema hit telling the story of someone's rise to success, an underdog overcoming adversity—*Rocky*, *The Karate Kid*, *One on One*, and virtually every sports film ever made. Or you may go the downhill route and write a story that's less popular but garners more critical respect. *All the King's Men. The Wolf of Wall Street.* This also includes novels like *The Ginger Man* and films like *Taxi Driver* that seem to portray the seamy side of success, individualism or heroism viewed without the rose-colored glasses.

The idea of separation and reunion appears nowhere so powerfully as it does in the many stories about leaving home, being forced from home, and returning home. The very notion triggers a feeling of warmth and nostalgia that may exceed the comfort the home provided in the first place. The first of these may have been *The Odyssey*, Ulysses' twenty-year (or more, depending upon how you translate it) journey home after the Trojan War to be reunited with his still-loyal and patiently awaiting wife. This theme has been taken up many times since, by *Cold Mountain* (allegedly based upon *The Odyssey*, though if so the author must have skipped the last chapter) and of course, the film version of *The Wizard of Oz* (was I the only kid who thought Dorothy was crazy to leave Oz for dreary Dust-Bowl Kansas?)?

As always, the stories that show us the dark side of the theme incur more critical respect. Thus, Thomas Wolfe told us that *You*

Can't Go Home Again. Because even if it looks good from a distance, it won't be when you get there. This is a variation on the old saws about being careful what you wish for, the grass is always greener on the other side, and so forth. There have been many stories addressing midlife crises, the feeling that one's life is meaningless or misdirected or wasted, such as *Death of a Salesman*, or more comically, *The Accidental Tourist*, or in the film world, *The Big Chill*. These characters find themselves a far cry from home, or from where they set out to be, and they aren't happy about it.

Everyone has felt separated from others, from the life they sought, from success, from the fundamental pleasures that give life meaning. That's what provides these stories such universal appeal. Even the dark stories can be seen as cautionary tales—don't do what this character did or you'll end up the same way. But most follow a more optimistic path. They point readers toward the light, at least as the writer perceives the light. They offer hope, redemption, second chances. They represent triumphs of the human spirit. Stories that key into this theme will always be popular, and there's no reason why you shouldn't write the next one.

ISOLATION VS. SOCIALIZATION

RELATIONSHIP STORIES HAVE ALWAYS BEEN THE MOST POPULAR, AND they probably always will be. You may have seen sneering stories noting that romances are the most popular genre. That was true in the paperback era and it continues to be true in the eBook era. Why are we surprised? Aren't relationships the core of every person's life? Romantic partners, business partners, parents, children, families, friends—it's all a variation on the larger theme of isolation vs. socialization, the complications involved in getting along with other people. It would be easier to be a hermit—and yet few are. Difficult or not, the search for others with whom to share your life seems eternal.

In *The Symposium*, Plato describes a theory that men and women were once united as one dual being, but Zeus split us, condemning us to spend the rest of our lives in search of our other halves. This was undoubtedly meant to explain the crazed lengths people go to in search of their soulmates. He's not the first to wonder what could possibly be the reason for so much bother. In his brilliant musical *Company*, Stephen Sondheim bucked decades of tradition by writing a musical that was all about relationships—but not all that romantic. Most musicals end with the central couple becoming lovers, and that constitutes a happy ending. Not *Company*. The show's protagonist, Bobby, ultimately concedes that although marriage is almost impossibly hard and endlessly trying, it is still better than being alone. We pair off, he sings in the finale, "...to help us survive...being alive."

Complicated relationships are not confined to marriage. In today's world, perhaps more than ever before, many find they don't have time for decent friendships, or worse, substitute virtual friendships, maintained through texting and selfies, for more meaningful relationships, leading to all-time high numbers for depression and teen suicide. Have you noticed that most successful sitcoms are about some group of loveable losers? *Friends. How I Met Your Mother. The Big Bang Theory.* The appeal is obvious. As flawed or downright stupid as the characters may appear, everyone wishes they had a group of steady friends like that. Because so few today do.

Relationships provide an endless bounty of theme.

Is it any wonder that the theme of isolation vs. socialization, the trauma of being alone vs. the trauma of having to deal with others, occupies so much fictional time? Sartre famously wrote (in *No Exit*) "Hell is other people," but I can't help but note that he had romantic relationships, adopted a daughter, taught classes, and had many professional and social acquaintances. A love-hate relationship with the rest of humanity has fueled more than a few stories. Because love, in all its forms and varieties, is the most powerful bond that ever existed between people. And many spend much of their time in pursuit of it.

The most obvious example of this theme would be, well, every romance novel ever written. Whether you're talking about *Jane Eyre* or the Harlequin romances that used to fill the grocery store racks, the basic theme is of love gained, and the reassuring message is that your soulmate is indeed out there. There are almost as many tales of love lost, often romanticizing a painful situation to such a degree that it seems more wonderful to lose love than to have a successful relationship. When I grew up, everyone read *Love Story*. More recently, it was *The Bridges of Madison County*. In the film world, *Casablanca* and *Annie Hall* leap to mind. Dare I add *Fifty Shades of Grey* to this list? Despite the unconventional sex, it is essentially a romance, a Cinderella story for an era less ashamed about what they do behind closed doors.

Closely related to this would be heroic tales about people making sacrifices in the name of love. *A Tale of Two Cities*. *City Lights* (the best movie ever). *Forrest Gump*. On the flip side, there are darker tales of love gone wrong, or selfish love, or love leading to disastrous consequences. You can trace this theme all the way from *Othello* to *Gone with the Wind*. Parental love, the strains in relations between fathers and sons, mothers and daughters, constantly occurs in fiction—because it constantly occurs in real life. *Fathers and Sons*. *Kramer vs. Kramer*. *Lorenzo's Oil*—and almost every contemporary young adult novel set in the real world.

In children's fiction, the love for pets and other animals recurs with great frequency. *Black Beauty*. *The Black Stallion*. *The Yearling*. *Old Yeller*. *Free Willy*. *Marley & Me*. Was I surprised when a poem I wrote about my cat turned out to be the most popular poem in my first book of poetry? If I was, I shouldn't have been.

Who hasn't loved and lost a pet? When you zero in on these universal touchstones, you may ignite an emotional firestorm in the reader's mind.

People tend to want the same things, chase the same goals, and believe the same truths. This is why we have universal themes that recur in fiction, and this is why understanding those themes—and employing them—can make your work so much more powerful. Emphasizing the positive side of the theme may encourage warmth or nostalgia. Going the other direction may trigger long-buried fears. But what is essential is that you cause the reader to feel something, that you stir emotions, which in turn will spur thoughts. When you cause readers to reexamine themselves, their lives, and their place in society, you start a chain reaction that is the hallmark of books that survive the test of time and leave a deep and abiding imprint on their readers. Perhaps, as I suggest in the next chapter, you may write something that changes more than mere minds. You might even change the world.

HIGHLIGHTS/EXERCISES

Highlights

1) The micro-theme is a specific topic for consideration. The macro-theme is a universal theme that relates to the human condition.

2) All themes fall into one of three universal categories, the conflicts between: 1) survival vs. extinction; 2) separation vs. reunion, and 3) isolation vs. socialization.

3) Survival themes may address the continued existence of the species, a discrete group, or even an individual.

4) The longing for connection and meaning is the source of endless thematic material.

5) Relationships provide an endless bounty of theme.

Red Sneaker Exercises

1) The previous chapters must have triggered some thoughts about what theme you are writing, or might like to write in the future. Now you should think about what larger macro-theme your theme fits under. Finding the right umbrella might enrich the theme and help you write about it without being obvious. What is the core idea or emotion in your work? The longing for something lost? The search for the other half? The innate desire for survival?

2) Sometimes even the best apocalyptic novels are not so much about the SF threat as they are about humans dealing with the before or after. One of the most powerful films ever made about the nuclear-war threat was *The Day After*, Nicholas Meyer's bleak saga of families trying to survive in a world where life has become not worth the trouble. One of my favorite films is *Last Night*. In that one, we're never told what will cause the world to end, but it's going to and everyone knows it. How they face that final curtain provides some wonderful moments of insightful characterization. Sometimes we see what characters are really made of when circumstances are most desperate. Can you use your survival theme to tell a story that provides greater insight into the human condition?

3) What has been the most powerful relationship in your life? Don't jump to easy or obvious answers. It may be a parent. It may be a spouse. It may be a dog. Or it may be none of the above. Be honest with yourself. What has it been in your life? How can you instill a relationship of equal importance in the life of your protagonist—and what thematic suggestion will you be making if you do?

7

WRITING FOR CHANGE

"The greatest art in the world is the art of storytelling."

— CECIL B. DEMILLE

There are many reasons a writer may decide to write. Some claim they started because they needed cash—though there are far more reliable means of getting it than a career in the arts. Fame? Books are still the most influential of the arts, I believe, but unquestionably more media attention is given to actors (people who memorize words written for them by writers). Some people have the unquenchable urge to tell a story, to entertain. And there are those who have something to say, a viewpoint to express, a point to make. These are the people who want to change the world—with words. It has been done before and will be done again. Maybe the next person who pulls it off will be you.

If you have a message and the story is in complete service to that message, you're writing an allegory, and frankly, are unlikely to find much success in the modern literary marketplace. I hope I've made it clear why it is better to be subtle, to avoid being preachy. Don't be a scold. Don't take the attitude that you know more about this than anyone else. That's a sure turnoff. Instead, assume that your readers are intelligent people (because why else would they be reading a book?) and that they must be somewhat interested in your subject or they wouldn't be reading your work. People read because they want to learn, they want to know more. At all costs, avoid arrogance. If you're worried that a passage or line of dialogue might seem sanctimonious or preachy—then it probably does. Cut it out and try a fresh approach.

This does not mean you have to water down what you want to say. Go large or go home, right? Never worry that your book might offend someone. If your book doesn't offend anyone, you haven't said anything. Some authors brag about having perfect five-star Amazon reviews. If I see a review page for one of my books with no dissenting opinions, I know I haven't said anything that mattered, anything that challenged anyone. I'd rather have my average dragged down by someone who was deeply offended by my book. At least then I'd know I've been doing my job.

Don't be preachy, but don't be afraid to tell the truth.

There are subtler ways to wreak change. Instead of avoiding difficult truths, consider your presentation. Think about balance, presenting both sides. Think about timing. I titled this book "Thinking Theme" for several reasons. Obviously, the pattern in this series has been to employ two-word alliterative titles, so why stop now? This title is basically "Thinking About Theme" with the middle word omitted. But that omission permits another interpretation, because what all these chapters have guided you toward is the construction of a "thinking theme," that is, a theme that provokes thinking, that reflects thinking, that elevates a story that might otherwise seem less important. In a world in which more books are churned out each month than most people could read in a lifetime, a thinking theme may be what distinguishes your work from the others.

. . .

The Reader as Traveling Companion

In the world of writing, you hear a lot of talk about journeys. The protagonist is on a journey, and perhaps other characters are journeying. Some people have written about the artist's journey. Christopher Vogler has written a fine book called *The Writer's Journey*. But what I want you to consider now is that you are taking your reader on a journey. And by that, I don't simply mean that you are entertaining them for a brief time. I mean that you are taking them on a voyage of discovery. If you allow them to discover your theme as your protagonist does, they will arrive there naturally, without feeling they have been led by the nose. And that's when you are most likely to inspire change.

Take your reader on a voyage.

You may have noticed that most of the five character arcs describe a journey. In the most popular of them, the coming-of-age plot, you start with a character whose ideas are not yet fully formed. This allows you to chart their journey, marking the signposts, the character turning points. If your story involves a theme of prejudice or injustice, you will probably plant scenes along the way that illustrate the wrongs of the world, exposing the protagonist to them. The hero's education, therefore, becomes the reader's education. This is what Harriet Beecher Stowe did so well in *Uncle Tom's Cabin*. She skipped the lectures and instead showed Eliza and Eva and Tom and the others victimized by the cruelties of slavery. She took her readers on a journey, and most arrived at the same destination—a conviction that slavery could no longer be tolerated by a civilized society.

One of the hardest journeys for me to chart was in one of the early books in the Kincaid series, *Perfect Justice*. Ben is vacationing in Arkansas and becomes embroiled in a conflict between

Vietnamese immigrants and a local hate group. The theme of prejudice is central to the story. The obvious journey would've been to have right-thinking Ben Kincaid disapprove of those hateful people, march in and set things straight. So I didn't do that. Instead, I had Ben embody another important idea—everyone is entitled to a fair trial. He notes that no one wants to represent the hatemonger accused of murder, the public defender is incompetent and scared, and the only way this man will get a fair trial is if Ben handles it himself—even though the man repulses him. That gave rise to a story that still embodied the central theme but was unexpected, unpredictable. The reader is still on a journey but one that seems less polemical or obvious. And as the story proceeds, the evils of prejudice—even prejudice against an unsympathetic racist—are thoroughly dramatized.

The Evil of Arrogance

ONE OF THE REASONS PREACHINESS IS SO OFF-PUTTING IS THAT IT almost always comes across as arrogant. People are rarely persuaded of anything by those who seem smug or too self-assured. Why do they need us? They've got their own built-in support staff in the form of a gigantic ego. People who think they have it all figured out, who brook no new ideas or outside input, are simply unbearable and rarely have much positive impact on the world.

Arrogance is irritating.

This is yet another reason for keeping your thematic ideas on the down low, under the surface of the story. Instead of giving in to arrogance, try a more self-deprecating approach. Don't act as if you have all the answers. Put the topic up for consideration, without skewering it in advance. Readers are more likely to be persuaded by ideas they believe they've discovered on their own.

The Adventures of Huckleberry Finn is, as I mentioned earlier, one of the great American novels. In this wonderful book, Huck is on a voyage of discovery. The primary conflict is between the socially accepted idea that slavery is desirable and the radical notion that it is not. Spending time with Jim helps Huck understand that there is something problematic about enslaving others, despite what his high society mentors say. And yet, he never announces a conclusion or suggests that he has all the answers. In the famous final passage, he tells the reader, "But I reckon I got to light out for the Territory ahead of the rest, because Aunt Sally she's going to adopt me and sivilize me and I can't stand it. I been there before." Most readers perceive this as an implicit, non-intellectual rejection of the ways of civilization—including slavery. The journey has led to a conclusion, even if the conclusion is never specifically announced as such.

But What Am I Supposed to Do About It?

IN SOME LITERARY CIRCLES, THE BLEAK, HOPELESS ENDING IS perceived as being more sophisticated, even more realistic, than the upbeat optimistic ending. I'm not sure why this is, or what is says about us, or critics, or academia. I'm just reporting the facts. Let me urge you against this approach unless you truly believe it is the best, perhaps only, credible way to conclude your story. I'm not saying every story should lead to some ridiculous Disney happy ending. I am saying there is little value in leaving your reader feeling bleak or depressed. Is that an appropriate reward for having journeyed with you for so many pages? You don't need to have everything work out perfectly or to suggest that the characters will all live happily ever after. But you should create some kind of positive takeaway. Students read books by nihilists and existentialists when they are assigned in classes, but can you honestly say they have made a profound impact? Readers are far more likely to be inspired by an ending that suggests hope than an ending that suggests futility.

Don't leave your readers with a feeling of hopelessness.

Writing about problems doesn't accomplish much if your ultimate message is that the struggle is pointless, especially if the problem is one that is already with us, has always been with us, and likely will always be with us. There may be some value in cautionary tales. Most of George Orwell's work is designed to warn us about the hideousness of life under Communism (*Animal Farm*) or a totalitarian government (*1984*). Since this had not occurred yet in the Western world, there was value in suggesting that we should resist it at all costs, whatever the short-term advantages might be. More recent works have extolled the values of maintaining the historic American dedication to privacy, even though we might be better able to defend against terrorists and crazed snipers if we allowed government agencies to eavesdrop on private conversations and search homes without a warrant. Warnings about the dangers of possible future dystopias have been a fixture in science fiction, especially alternate or parallel universe stories.

Even when you are addressing matters of great import, instead of suggesting hopelessness, try to suggest a possible remedy. Sound a call for action. It doesn't have to be obvious. You don't need to put an electronic petition at the end of the eBook. But suggesting a better way, a sounder course, a path out of the darkness, will lead to a more positive and ultimately more useful book. It is also more likely to be treasured and recommended by readers, because after all, once you have helped them see the correct path, they will want to share it with others.

Leave your readers with a call for action.

I mentioned before some of the occasions when readers have said my work changed the way they saw the world. Those are some of my most treasured letters from readers. But there is another I treasure even more. This letter came all the way from Ireland, from a young man who was in a mental institution because he had become a danger to himself. He suffered from depression and bipolar disorder and a host of other ailments. At first they did not allow him to read fiction, but when they did, against all odds, a nurse offered him my book *Capitol Murder*. He liked it and looked for more in the series. He read them and liked them, one after another. He wrote to thank me, saying that my stories, following Ben Kincaid on his quests for justice, helped him get through a difficult time in his life, and that he would always be grateful for that.

You can probably see why this is my favorite letter. You can probably also see that this would never have happened if I had ended the books on a bleak, depressing, note. I try to keep those novels squarely within the real world. But at the same time, Ben typically finds some measure of imperfect justice even in an imperfect world, and he never gives up, just as we should never give up. He is an optimistic figure, and although I avoid making the books formulaic or predictable, he will always be an optimistic figure.

Suggest optimism rather than pessimism.

Books are the light that never dies. Whether you are a lonely child seeking refuge in the local library, a troubled soul in a psychiatric ward, or a regular person with a job, spouse, and kids, the best books will offer you direction, a glimpse of something better. We live in an age of negativity, short attention spans, and purposelessness. Nonfiction books have been written to help people find purpose, but perhaps you can, in your fiction, suggest a path in a far subtler, and thus more penetrating, way.

You will not be the first idealistic soul to use fiction as a means to bring about change. Neither was Harriet Beecher Stowe. Thoreau's *On Civil Disobedience* is not exactly a story, but it is written work that wrought profound change, influencing Gandhi and Martin Luther King, Jr, and reshaping the modern world. Rachel Carson launched the environmental movement with a book. Upton Sinclair reformed the meat packing industry. *Things Fall Apart* by Chinua Achebe turned the world against colonialism. *The Ragged Trousered Philanthropists* by Robert Tressell, dramatizing the downside of capitalism, led to many social reforms. *All Quiet on the Western Front* forged many a pacifist in the fires of its turbulent drama. Toni Morrison's *Beloved* brought the evils of racism, the plight of a young black woman, to life in a way that continues to haunt many readers. In the nineteenth century, Dickens' stories repeatedly wrought contemporary legal reforms that benefitted students, orphans, and the poor.

Books have changed the world. For the better. And they will again.

Choose your themes wisely. Bring them to life on the page. Then sit back and watch what happens.

HIGHLIGHTS/EXERCISES

Highlights

1) Don't be preachy, but don't be afraid to tell the truth.

2) Take your reader on a voyage.

3) Arrogance is irritating.

4) Don't leave your readers with a feeling of hopelessness.

5) Leave your readers with a call for action.

6) Always suggest optimism rather than pessimism.

7) Books have changed the world—and will again.

Red Sneaker Exercises

1) Which one of the world's current problems—and let's face it, there are many to choose from—concerns you the most? Do you

have any ideas about what course of action, what change in attitude, what spirit of cooperation or selflessness, might make the problem better? Is there a way to address this in your book, without becoming overtly political or preachy?

2) If you have a specific thematic goal in mind, and it's at all controversial (and if it isn't, why bother writing about it?) then you must realize there will be some opposition. Can you head that off at the pass? Can you dramatize the likely results of what you perceive as the wrong course of action, in the manner that Orwell dramatized the end result of government seeking greater control, or Huxley dramatized the end result of a population always in pursuit of pleasure?

3) If you're writing a coming-of-age story, can you explore your chosen topic and theme through the experiences your protagonist has on the journey from inciting incident to climax? Let the readers' eyes be opened at the same time that it happens to your fictional character. In terms of plotting, you generally outline so the plot represents a series of increasingly difficult obstacles. Let your character (and reader's) education take the shape of increasingly powerful images and events.

APPENDIX A: THE THEMATIC CHECKLIST

In this chart I've identified some of the most frequently recurring micro-themes and organized them in terms of their corresponding macro-theme. Most of the examples are discussed in the text. Which category best serves your purposes, or best corresponds with the story you want to write? How can you achieve the success of the works mentioned in this list? How can you give your approach a fresh spin?

Survival vs. Extinction

Prejudice: *To Kill a Mockingbird, The Color Purple, Philadelphia, The Help, Beloved*

War: *All Quiet on the Western Front, Platoon, Full Metal Jacket, Dunkirk, The Hunger Games*

Dehumanization: *Brave New World, Fahrenheit 451, 1984, Modern Times, The Terminator*

Injustice: *Twelve Angry Men, The Fugitive*, the Ben Kincaid series, *In the Name of the Father, The Verdict*

Conspiracies: *The Da Vinci Code, The Manchurian Candidate, Three Days of the Condor, All the President's Men*

Obsession: *Moby Dick, American Beauty, Fatal Attraction, Star Trek II: The Wrath of Khan*

Corruption: *Macbeth, The Treasure of the Sierra Madre, Wall Street, Citizen Kane, Amadeus*

Separation vs. Reunion

Alienation: *Taxi Driver, Easy Rider, Citizen Kane, Alice's Restaurant, The Great Gatsby*

Returning Home: *The Odyssey, Cold Mountain, The Wizard of Oz, O Brother, Where Art Thou?, You Can't Go Home Again*

Underdogs: *Rocky, The Karate Kid*, Horatio Alger stories, the Ben Kincaid series, *The Firm, A Tale of Two Cities*

Rebellion: *One Flew Over the Cuckoo's Nest, Braveheart, Gandhi, Selma, Woodstock, The Adventures of Huckleberry Finn*

Redemption: *Lord Jim, A Christmas Carol, In the Line of Fire, The Verdict*

Life Crises: *Death of a Salesman, The Accidental Tourist, The Big Chill, The Man in the Gray Flannel Suit*

Isolation vs. Socialization

Love Gained: *When Harry Met Sally, Beauty and the Beast, Continental Divide, Somewhere in Time*, every romance novel ever

Love Lost: *Romeo and Juliet, Love Story, Casablanca, Annie Hall, Manhattan*

Selfless Love: *City Lights, Forrest Gump, Casablanca, The Best Years of Our Lives*

Selfish Love: *Othello, Fatal Attraction, Gone with the Wind*

Friendship: *Three Men in a Boat, E.T., Midnight Cowboy, Lethal Weapon, Thelma and Louise*

Parental Love: *Fathers and Sons, Kramer vs. Kramer, Lorenzo's Oil, Mildred Pierce, Stella Dallas, Mommie Dearest*

Animal Love: *Black Beauty, The Black Stallion, The Yearling, Free Willy*

APPENDIX B: THE WRITER'S CALENDAR

Is it possible to finish a top-quality manuscript in six months? Of course it is, if you're willing to do the work necessary to make it happen. Here's how you do it.

Week 1

Commit to your writing schedule.

Find your writing place.

Inform friends and family that you are undertaking a major project and you would like their support.

Consider what you want to write. Start thinking like a writer.

Week 2

Commit to a premise—then make it bigger. Is it big and unique enough to attract a publisher?

Commit to a genre. What's your spin on the genre? How will you make it the same—but different? Research as needed.

Week 3

Develop your main protagonist and antagonist.

What are their best qualities—and worst? What drives them?

What is your protagonist's character arc? What does he/she want, seek, desire?

Write a half-page example of dialogue for each major character in their distinct voice.

Week 4

Put all major events (scenes) on index cards, approximately sixty total.

Arrange cards by acts. Highlight the Plot Turning Points and Character Turning Points.

Type the index cards into an outline, adding detail when you have it.

Week 5

Think about the shape of your story—the Plot. Will your character experience positive growth or maturation? Redemption? Disillusionment?

Map out twists and turns to maintain reader interest. What is the last twist the reader will suspect?

Don't shy away from a great scene because it doesn't fit your story as you currently understand it. See if you can change the story to accommodate the great scene.

Weeks 6-18

Write at least five pages every day—ten on Saturdays. No editing. Just keep moving ahead.

Do additional writing as necessary to complete 10 % of the book each week.

Week 19-23

Perform triage on what you've written. Revise. Then revise more. Focus on character consistency, character depth. Are the characters sympathetic or empathetic?

Focus on plot, pacing, story logic, theme. Is the story plausible?

Week 24-26

Give the manuscript to trusted reader(s).

Obtain comments from readers. Incorporate comments from readers where appropriate.

Set it aside for a time, then reread it with fresh eyes. Do you see problems you didn't spot before?

And then—

Attend writing conferences and bounce your ideas off agents and editors. If people don't ask to see your manuscript, your premise needs work. If people ask to see pages but don't take you on, it suggests your manuscript is not yet ready. Consider attending a small-group writing retreat to give your book that final push it needs to be publishable.

APPENDIX C: THE WRITER'S CONTRACT

Okay, you have a theme in mind, something important you want to convey in a story. Commit to getting the job done. Sign this contract. Get the rest of the family to sign as witnesses.

I, _____, hereinafter known as "the Writer," in consideration of these premises, hereby agree as follows:

1. Because I have something to say and I want readers to hear it, the aforementioned Writer will undertake a long-term, intensive writing project. The Writer agrees to work ___ hours a day, regardless of external distractions or personal circumstances. The Writer agrees to maintain this schedule until the writing project is completed.
2. The Writer understands that this is a difficult task and that there will be days when he/she does not feel like writing or when others make demands upon the Writer's writing time. The Writer will not allow this to interfere with the completion of the agreement made in paragraph one (1) of this contract.

3. The Writer also understands that good physical and mental health is essential to the completion of any writing project. Therefore, in order to complete the agreement made in paragraph one (1), the Writer commits to a serious program of self-care, which shall include but shall not be limited to: adequate sleep, healthy diet, exercise, the relinquishment of bad habits, and reading time.

_____

Signature of the Writer and Witnesses

APPENDIX D: GREAT LINES SUGGEST GREAT THEMES

Notice how many times these memorable lines from great novels steer the reader toward the theme.

It was the best of times, it was the worst of times, it was the age of wisdom, it was the age of foolishness, it was the epoch of belief, it was the epoch of incredulity, it was the season of Light, it was the season of Darkness, it was the spring of hope, it was the winter of despair, we had everything before us, we had nothing before us, we were all going direct to Heaven, we were all going direct the other way – in short, the period was so far like the present period, that some of its noisiest authorities insisted on its being received, for good or for evil, in the superlative degree of comparison only. —Charles Dickens, *A Tale of Two Cities*

Fate is like a strange, unpopular restaurant, filled with odd waiters who bring you things you never asked for and don't always like. —Lemony Snicket

Life isn't about what happens to you, it's about how you handle what happens. —Nicholas Evans, *The Smoke Jumper*

Death is but the next great adventure. —Albus Dumbledore (J.K. Rowling) (*Harry Potter and the Sorcerer's Stone*)

And I, of course, am innocent of all but malice. —Fiona, *Sign of the Unicorn*, Roger Zelazny

And if you're going to criticize me for not finishing the whole thing and tying it up in a bow for you, why, do us both a favor and write your own damn book, only have the decency to call it a romance instead of a history, because history's got no bows on it, only frayed ends of ribbons and knots that can't be untied. It ain't a pretty package, but then it's not your birthday that I know of so I'm under no obligation to give you a gift. —Orson Scott Card, *Alvin Journeyman*

Because we are the people, and the people go on. —Ma Joad, *The Grapes of Wrath*, John Steinbeck

Death belongs to God alone. By what right do men touch that unknown thing? —Victor Hugo, *Les Misérables*

Life is a Gift Horse. —J.D. Salinger, *Teddy*

Life is pain. Anybody that says different is selling something. —Fezzik's mother, *The Princess Bride*

Not all who wander are lost. —J.R.R. Tolkien, *The Fellowship of the Ring*

The surest sign that there is intelligent life elsewhere in the universe is that none of it has tried to contact us. —*Calvin and Hobbes*

A bore is a person who deprives you of solitude without providing you with company. —John MacDonald, *The Turquoise Lament*

All animals are equal, but some are more equal than others. —George Orwell, *Animal Farm*

Behind them lay pain, and death, and fear. Ahead of them lay doubt, and danger, and fathomless mysteries. But they weren't alone. —Philip Pullman, *The Golden Compass*

Certain things should just stay as they are. You ought to be able to stick them in one of those big glass cases and just leave them alone. —JD Salinger, *Catcher in the Rye*

Dad, how do soldiers killing each other solve the world's problems? —*Calvin and Hobbes*

APPENDIX E: THE RED SNEAKER WRITER'S READING LIST

The Chicago Manual of Style. 16th ed. Chicago: University of Chicago Press, 2010.

Cook, Vivian. *All in a Word: 100 Delightful Excursions into the Uses and Abuses of Words.* Brooklyn: Melville House, 2010.

Fowler, H.W. *Fowler's Modern English Usage.* 3rd ed. Rev. Ernest Gowers. N.Y. & Oxford: Oxford University Press, 2004.

Goldman, William. *Adventures in the Screen Trade: A Personal View of Hollywood and Screenwriting.* New York: Grand Central, 1989.

Hale, Constance. *Sin and Syntax: How to Create Wickedly Effective Prose.* New York: Broadway Books, 2001.

Hart, Jack. *A Writer's Coach: The Complete Guide to Writing Strategies That Work.* New York: Anchor Books, 2006.

Jones, Catherine Ann. *The Way of Story: The Craft and Soul of Writing.* Studio City: Michael Wiese Productions, 2007.

Klauser, Henriette Anne. *Writing on Both Sides of the Brain.* San Francisco: Harper & Row, 1987.

Maass, Donald. *The Fire in Fiction: Passion, Purpose, and Techniques to Make Your Novel Great.* Cincinnati: Writers Digest Books, 2009.

Maass, Donald. *Writing the Breakout Novel: Insider Advice for Taking Your Fiction to the Next Level*. Cincinnati: Writers Digest Books, 2001.

Maass, Donald. *Writing 21st Century Fiction: High Impact Techniques for Exceptional Storytelling*. Cincinnati: Writers Digest Books, 2012.

O'Conner, Patricia T. *Woe Is I: The Grammarphobe's Guide to Better English in Plain English*. 2nd ed. New York: Riverhead Books, 2003.

O'Conner, Patricia T. *Origins of the Specious: Myths and Misconceptions of the English Language*. New York: Random House, 2009.

Strunk, William, Jr., and White, E.B. *The Elements of Style*. 4th ed. N.Y.: Macmillan, 2000.

Truss, Lynne. *Eats Shoots & Leaves: The Zero Tolerance Guide to Punctuation*. New York: Gotham Books, 2005.

Vogler, Christopher. *The Writer's Journey: Mythic Structure for Storytellers and Screenwriters*. Studio City: Michael Wiese Productions, 1992.

Zinsler, William. *On Writing Well: The Classic Guide to Writing Nonfiction*. 30th Anniv. Ed. New York: Harper Perennial, 2006.

ABOUT THE AUTHOR

William Bernhardt is the author of forty-nine books, including *The Last Chance Lawyer (#1 Bestseller)*, the historical novels *Challengers of the Dust* and *Nemesis*, two books of poetry, and the Red Sneaker books on fiction writing. In addition, Bernhardt founded the Red Sneaker Writers Center to mentor aspiring author. The Center hosts an annual conference (WriterCon), small-group seminars, a newsletter, a phone app, and a bi-weekly podcast. He is also the owner of Balkan Press, which publishes poetry and fiction as well as the literary journal *Conclave*.

Bernhardt has received the Southern Writers Guild's Gold Medal Award, the Royden B. Davis Distinguished Author Award (University of Pennsylvania) and the H. Louise Cobb Distinguished Author Award (Oklahoma State), which is given "in recognition of an outstanding body of work that has profoundly influenced the way in which we understand ourselves and American society at large." In 2019, he received the Arrell Gibson Lifetime Achievement Award from the Oklahoma Center for the Book.

In addition Bernhardt has written plays, a musical (book and score), humor, children stories, biography, and puzzles. He has edited two anthologies (*Legal Briefs* and *Natural Suspect*) as fundraisers for The Nature Conservancy and the Children's Legal Defense Fund. In his spare time, he has enjoyed surfing, digging for dinosaurs, trekking through the Himalayas, paragliding, scuba diving, caving, zip-lining over the canopy of the Costa Rican rain forest, and jumping out of an airplane at 10,000 feet.

In 2017, when Bernhardt delivered the keynote address at the

San Francisco Writers Conference, chairman Michael Larsen noted that in addition to penning novels, Bernhardt can "write a sonnet, play a sonata, plant a garden, try a lawsuit, teach a class, cook a gourmet meal, beat you at Scrabble, and work the *New York Times* crossword in under five minutes."

For more information
www.williambernhardt.com
wb@williambernhardt.com

AUTHOR'S NOTE

Watch for the next volume in the Red Sneaker Writers Book series.

Would you consider posting a review of this book online? I'd really appreciate it. I hope you'll also consider reading some of my fiction, including the Daniel Pike novels, starting with *The Last Chance Lawyer.*

Please consider attending WriterCon over Labor Day weekend in Oklahoma City. For more information, visit www.writercon.org. If you're interested in attending one of my small-group writing retreats, visit my webpage.

Need some feedback on your writing? Check out my Patreon page at https://www.patreon.com/willbern

I publish a free e-newsletter on a regular basis. The Red Sneaker Writers Newsletter is for writers and aspiring writers, filled with market and writing news. You can sign up at my website. There's also a bi-weekly Red Sneakers podcast, available everywhere you get podcasts.

For more information, please visit my website at http://www.williambernhardt.com. You can email me at willbern@gmail.com.

Made in the USA
Monee, IL
05 March 2021